THE HIDING PLACE

The Hiding Place © 2022 by A. S. Peterson

Published by
Rabbit Room Press
3321 Stephens Hill Lane
Nashville, Tennessee 37013
info@rabbitroom.com

All rights reserved. No portion of this book may be reproduced, stored in a retrieval system, hidden in a secret room, or transmitted in any form or by any means—electronic, mechanical, photocopy, recording, scanning, telegraph, or other—except for brief quotations in critical reviews or articles, without the prior written permission of the publisher.

Performance rights are neither granted nor implied.
Contact info@rabbitroom.com for information on performance rights.

Version 1.1

ISBN: 9781732691087

RABBIT ROOM THEATRE
PRESENTS

CORRIE TEN BOOM'S
THE HIDING PLACE

STAGEPLAY BY A. S. PETERSON

Adapted from the book
by Corrie ten Boom
with Elizabeth and John Sherrill

THE HIDING PLACE was commissioned and given its world premiere in Houston, Texas, by A. D. Players (Jake Speck, Executive Director; Kevin Dean, Artistic Director). Performances began September 11, 2019 in the George Theater.

In 2022 the play underwent revision and was re-staged in Nashville, Tennessee, by Rabbit Room Theatre.

Also by A. S. PETERSON

FIN'S REVOLUTION

BOOK 1: THE FIDDLER'S GUN
"A soulful, instant classic."
—Allan Heinberg, Screenwriter of WONDER WOMAN

BOOK 2: FIDDLER'S GREEN
"Inventive, engaging, unpredictable. Peterson's prose sparkles with life."
—Douglas McKelvey, author of EVERY MOMENT HOLY

THE BATTLE OF FRANKLIN
STAGEPLAY
"A true poet, Peterson's language is rich with imagery."
—Amy Stumpfl, THE TENNESSEAN

FRANKENSTEIN
STAGEPLAY
"Provocative and mesmerizing in the scope of its storytelling."
--Jeffrey Ellis, BROADWAY WORLD

TALES OF AN UNREMEMBERED COUNTRY
THE TIMELY ARRIVAL OF BARNABAS BEAD

THE ORACLE OF PHILADELPHIA

CAST

CORRIE TEN BOOM (50s) – A middle-aged woman. Sister of Betsie and Willem. Daughter of Casper (red patch while in prison).

CASPER TEN BOOM (70s) – An elderly man

BETSIE TEN BOOM (50s) – A middle-aged woman. Throughout the play, she wears some piece of bright green clothing (red patch while in prison).

WILLEM TEN BOOM (40s) – An eager and serious man

LT. RICHTER (30s–40s) – A Nazi interrogator

OTTO SCHWARZHUBER (20s) – A rude young German

PICKWICK (40s–50s) – A Dutch politician who runs the underground resistance. He is rotund, polite, and jolly.

FRED KOORNSTRA (40s–50s) – A Dutch man who works in the Food Office

SOLDIER 1 & 2 – Nazi soldiers

MARY ITALLIE (60s) – A sickly, elderly, Jewish woman

MEYER MOSSEL (30–40s) – An amiable Jewish man

META MONSANTO (40s) – A Jewish woman

THEA DACOSTA (40s) – A Jewish woman

HENK (30s–40s) – A Jewish man

Workman 1 & 2

Gita – A Polish woman imprisoned at Ravensbruck (red patch)

Jeske – A Dutch woman imprisoned at Ravensbruck (black patch)

Avien (8–10) – Jeske's daughter (black patch)

Trudka – A Polish woman imprisoned at Ravensbruck (red patch)

Prisoners – Male and female prisoners (colors in a prisoners name denote the color of patch they wear)

Guard 1 & 2 – Female/male Nazi guards at Ravensbruck

The Beast – A female guard and overseer at Ravensbruck

Moorman (30s–40s) – A prisoner functionary who oversees other prisoners (red patch)

Jewish Couple – Refugees

German Overseer – A Nazi officer in charge of factory production

German Officer – A Nazi who leads the raid on the Beje

Red Cross Worker 1 & 2 – Workers who rescue Corrie and liberate Ravensbruck

Nurse – a Nazi infirmary worker

Train Attendant – a ticket-taker

Young Corrie (8–10)

Young Betsie (8–10)

Company – During some scenes, company members will comprise the townspeople of Haarlem, the prisoners aboard the train, and the prisoners at Ravensbruck.

SUGGESTED TRACKS:

CORRIE
BETSIE
CASPER
PICKWICK / GUARD 2
OTTO / PRISONER RED
WILLEM / JEWISH PRISONER / RED CROSS WORKER 2
LT. RICHTER / RED CROSS WORKER 1 / MALE PRISONER GREEN 2
HENK / SOLDIER 2 / WORKMAN 2 / GERMAN OVERSEER
THEA / JESKE / JEWISH WOMAN
MEYER / MOORMAN / TRAIN ATTENDANT
FRED KOORNSTRA / GERMAN OFFICER / GUARD 1
TRUDKA / FEMALE PRIONER BLACK
MARY ITALLIE / PRISONER 1 / GITA
JEWISH WOMAN / PRISONER 1 / FEMALE PRISONER BLACK / NURSE
WORKMAN 1 / JEWISH MAN / MALE PRISONER GREEN 1 / SOLDIER 1
META / THE BEAST / NURSE
AVIEN / YOUNG BETSIE
YOUNG CORRIE

*NOTE: Prisoner names that include a color are to indicate which color patch that prisoner wears.

PRODUCTION NOTES:

In Act 1, the set requires an area for the watch shop, a wall and bed to form the "hiding place," and a table around which much of the action will happen. This table may serve as the dinner table, the interrogation table, the office desk, etc. At the end of Act 1, all set pieces are rolled away for effect and the train enters.

During Act 2, the set is comprised the prison barracks, the infirmary/factory, and the crematorium. An elevated pole is placed onstage for the torture of prisoners. The set during Act 2 is almost entirely devoid of color so that Betsie's green colors stand out when she is present or are noticeably absent when she is offstage. During most of Act 2, the smokestack looms above the prison crematorium and emits smoke, at times belching it in greater volume. The presence of the oven should be felt but not seen, until it is revealed in Act 2/Scene 6.

ACT I

SCENE 1

In front of the curtain, set in place before the audience has arrived, is a sturdy leather suitcase of considerable size. It sits alone and conspicuous and without explanation.

Lights down.

CORRIE enters, ignoring the suitcase. She considers the set as the lights reveal the Beje briefly, a Reich Flag briefly, a barracks, the great clock.

CORRIE: Listen. We are in the silence now. The silence between two ticks of the clock.

Listen.

Time is the canvas upon which the maker paints the strokes of his clock, and I have spent my life in the minutiae of its workings. Each piece spins and springs and lifts its hands to its maker. Each piece proclaiming in part what meaning can only be perceived in the unity of the whole.

Listen.

Justice. Suffering. Hope and Despair. Forgiveness and Despite. Their great engines are whirring all around us. And the more powerless one is to control them, the closer she is to the mystery that sets them in motion, draws them together, and makes of them something greater.

Listen.

It is mystery that loosens time's chains so that we may stand apart and apprehend realities more swift and vast than ever we dreamed. And so we are, perhaps, most wholly ourselves when viewed in all our times and places at once. The child. The woman. The daughter. The sister. The "watch woman." The . . . the . . . whatever it is she must become.

Listen with me now. Do you hear? The silence is ending. The chains begin to creak. The weights descend.

Watch.

The ticking of a great clock fills the Theater. The clock chimes once as the play begins.

Voices from offstage.

YOUNG CORRIE: Betsie, where have I put my shoes?

YOUNG BETSIE: Did you look in the parlor?

YOUNG CORRIE enters and rushes past CORRIE into the room.

YOUNG CORRIE: Papa! Papa? Where are you?

YOUNG BETSIE enters and puts on her coat.

YOUNG BETSIE: Be quiet, Corrie! Mama is sleeping.

YOUNG CORRIE: But Papa said we could go with him this morning. He hasn't left has he? It's still dark outside.

YOUNG BETSIE exits.

YOUNG CORRIE: Wait for me. Betsie!

YOUNG CORRIE exits as CORRIE looks on, astonished. The great clock strikes a chime and the ticking fades away.

A single, buzzing light flickers on, illuminating a table with a chair on either side.

CORRIE: What is this? Where am I? What's going on?

CORRIE looks around in confusion.

On the other side of the stage, another door opens. LT. RICHTER enters, sits, opens a briefcase, and methodically sets a collection of files on the table.

LT. RICHTER: Cornelia Arnolda Johanna ten Boom. Have I got that right?

Won't you sit? It's nearly spring. Did you know? The daffodils are peeking out. The tulips will be up before long.

Where did you say you were from?

CORRIE sits down.

LT. RICHTER: *(checking his files)*

Ah. Haarlem, yes? Not far from here.

CORRIE: Yes. Haarlem.

The great clock ticks. CASPER *entering, unseen by* RICHTER, *crossing upstage speaking as if to someone offstage.*

CASPER: Welcome to the Beje. Come in! Come in! Just a moment.

We have a customer! Willem! Corrie?

(winding his pocketwatch)

We have a train to catch, I'm afraid. Willem!

LT. RICHTER: I was in Haarlem only a few days ago. In fact, I returned with more bulbs than I had any right to.

I suspect my flower garden will get more out of this trip than the Reich will. Do you grow flowers, fraulein?

CORRIE: Yes. Well, no. My sister does, in windowboxes.

LT. RICHTER: Ah, yes. A sister. Let's see now. Elizabeth?

Ticking. YOUNG BETSIE *enters upstage.*

YOUNG BETSIE: Look, Corrie. It has to be buried before it can grow. We plant the bulb in the fall, and when spring comes, we'll have tulips.

CASPER: Thank you, Betsie. Will you go and fetch Willem for me?

YOUNG BETSIE: Yes, Papa.

Young Betsie places a pot on the sill of the shop window and exits.

CORRIE: Betsie.

LT. RICHTER: Yes, of course. Betsie. And where is she?

CORRIE: I don't know. I haven't seen her since . . .

LT. RICHTER: Yes. Since you arrived here.

And how long is that now?

CORRIE: One hundred and nineteen days.

LT. RICHTER: Hmmm. Then perhaps I can help you. Perhaps I can help your sister as well.

CORRIE: What about my father? Do you know where he is?

The ticking of the great clock. CASPER and YOUNG BETSIE enter followed by CORRIE. At times CORRIE speaks in place of YOUNG CORRIE.

YOUNG CORRIE: Papa, wait!

CASPER: I'm sorry, Corrie. But you must stay here to help your Tante Jans and Willem. Betsie will come with me this time.

YOUNG CORRIE: But she always gets to go! And I always get left behind! It's not fair!

YOUNG BETSIE: Papa, she can go in my place. I don't mind.

CASPER: No. Betsie, you will come with me, just as planned. Corrie, you must stay. I need you to see that the watches keep ticking and the light stays on when we're gone. Do you understand?

CORRIE: No, I don't.

YOUNG CORRIE: I want to come with you.

CASPER: I know you don't understand, but it's time to be a big girl now.

YOUNG CORRIE & CORRIE: But why!?

Beat.

CASPER: Do you see my suitcase over there? Bring it to me.

YOUNG CORRIE runs to the suitcase and tries to lift it but cannot. It's unnaturally heavy, as if it's attached to the stage.

YOUNG CORRIE: It's too heavy, Papa. I can't.

CASPER: No. You can't. And what kind of father would I be if I asked you to carry something you hadn't the strength to bear?

YOUNG CORRIE: I don't understand.

CASPER: I know. I know. But sometimes when you don't understand something, it's like that suitcase. It's too heavy, and you have to wait until you're bigger to lift it.

Do you see?

YOUNG CORRIE shakes her head sheepishly.

CASPER plucks the suitcase from the stage as if it weighs nothing at all.

CASPER: But you will, my little, Corrie. And until then you must trust that I love you.

Now then. Come along, Betsie. We've a train to catch, and Corrie has work to do.

Young Betsie and Casper exit. Young Corrie walks past Corrie. They exchange a look, then Young Corrie exits into shadow.

Lt. Richter: I will be truthful, fraulein. As I hope you will be with me.

                   We are aware of everything that's transpired in your home over the past two years. But we wish to obtain a proper record, you see? To put it in the proper order. And then, well, perhaps we can go back to tending our flowers.

Corrie: We've done nothing wrong.

Lt. Richter: Then come, fraulein. Tell me. What do you remember? Begin whenever you like.

Corrie stands and walks downstage. The ticking of a great clock swells.

The lights reveal the rest of the stage as Lt. Richter exits.

SCENE 2

The Beje, the Ten Boom house.

CORRIE: We were watchmakers. And watch-keepers. For a hundred years people brought their clocks and watches for the fixing.

The Beje shop is filled with clocks, and the air with their ticking. CASPER *enters and wanders the stage checking and winding them.*

CASPER: Ah, hah. No time to waste.

CASPER *checks his pocketwatch, raises a finger, and the clocks begin to chime at once.* CASPER *smiles in pleasure as* BETSIE *enters from the street with groceries from the market.*

BETSIE: My goodness, Papa! We'll wake the whole street.

CASPER: All in perfect synchronicity. Just as their makers intended.

The clocks finish chiming.

CASPER: Mister Janssen's was off by ten seconds but I've set it straight. Corrie, you'll have to keep an

	eye on it today. The rest are ready to go home, I think.
BETSIE:	While you two tend to your ticks and tocks, I'll get the coffee on and see if I can manage a breakfast to go with it.
CORRIE:	Did you see Pickwick this morning? His watch is ready to be picked up.
BETSIE:	I saw him, yes, but was helpless to distract him from the pastries in the Grote Market.
CASPER:	God help a pastry if that man is within a mile of it.
BETSIE:	Papa!
CORRIE:	Nevermind. I'm sure he'll be by later.

BETSIE exits. WILLEM bursts in the front door.

CORRIE:	Good morning, Willem!
CASPER:	Give your sister a kiss.
WILLEM:	Corrie.
CORRIE:	Have you left Tine at home again?
WILLEM:	I'm afraid so.
CORRIE:	I miss seeing her. You live too far away these days.
WILLEM:	The children talk about you all the time. "Where's Tante Corrie? I want Tante Corrie to tell me a story! Can we go visit Tante Corrie?"
CORRIE:	Do you hear that Papa? They miss me.

CASPER: What?

CORRIE: Nevermind.

WILLEM: Have you heard the radio this morning?

CORRIE: The radio? Why?

CASPER: What is it now?

WILLEM: First Poland, then Norway and Denmark. It's only a matter of time before we hear the boots of the Reich in Haarlem.

CASPER: They won't dare. They let us alone in the Great War, didn't they?

CORRIE: Let the big countries fight it out. It's no trouble of ours.

BETSIE enters.

BETSIE: Coffee is ready. Willem!

WILLEM: Coffee sounds marvelous.

BETSIE: Come in! There's breakfast if you'll stay.

WILLEM: I'd be glad of a bite, now that I think of it.

WILLEM *and* BETSIE *exit to the kitchen.* CASPER *goes to the radio and turns it on, tunes it. Hitler raves in German.* CASPER *and* CORRIE *listen a moment then* CASPER *turns the radio off.*

CORRIE: What if Willem is right?

CASPER: Hmm. Let us pray he is not.

CORRIE: Are you ever afraid, Papa?

CASPER: Afraid? Yes. But I wait for my ticket.

CORRIE: You wait for your what?

CASPER: My ticket!

CORRIE: What are you talking about?

CASPER: Let's eat some breakfast. No time to waste.

CORRIE and CASPER exit to the kitchen.

The breakfast table.

BETSIE: Sit down! Sit down!

CORRIE: Is this new, Betsie?

BETSIE: Isn't it something? Miss De Witte was going to toss out this lovely old swath of green. Can you imagine?

CASPER: That's my Betsie. Always keeping something from the fire.

WILLEM: She once turned one of my old shirts into a pillow. Do you remember?

CASPER: And now she's turned several of your pillows into my shirt.

CORRIE: Don't tease, Papa!

CASPER: Who says I'm teasing?

BETSIE: Coffee, all around then?

WILLEM: Please!

CASPER: Thank you, dear.

CORRIE: Fresh fruit from the market, bread from the oven, and a bit of Tante Jans' marmalade.

WILLEM: Now there's a reason to get up in the morning.

WILLEM reaches for the food but CASPER clears his throat.

CASPER: The food will be blessed first.

WILLEM: Of course, Papa.

CASPER: Lord, you know what makes the planets spin. You know what makes my watches hum. You set the atoms dancing. And in your grace you bless our feast with marmalade.

(to Corrie)

So tune our hearts to hear the tick and the tock of the vast engine of your mercy.

ALL: Amen.

The group eats.

BETSIE: What brings you to town this morning, Willem?

WILLEM: I have some news.

BETSIE: Isn't he coy about it?

CORRIE: Go on, then.

WILLEM: I'm leaving my position at the church.

BETSIE: What?

CORRIE: But how can you, Willem?

WILLEM: I think ministry is not my calling after all.

BETSIE: But what will you do?

WILLEM: I've opened a home for the elderly.

CASPER: The elderly?

WILLEM: There's a great need for it. There are more everyday who need help.

CORRIE: Well. This is a surprise.

BETSIE: But it's a good surprise. Right, Papa?

CASPER and WILLEM consider each other silently.

WILLEM: I'm sorry, Papa. But the Lord has called me to a new work.

CASPER: Then you are right to follow.

Besides, there are enough bad preachers in the world. The lessening of their ranks is indeed the Lord's work.

CORRIE: I'm telling Pastor Liam you said that.

CASPER: Well someone ought to.

BETSIE: Corrie and I must come and visit!

WILLEM: Then you'd best come quickly. Soon we'll have no beds left.

CORRIE: So many?

WILLEM: Fleeing Germany. They despise the elderly there. And many are Jews.

CASPER: Germany. Germany! Must we always gnaw on a single bone? It's all anyone will talk about. On

	the radio. In the newspapers. Even at my own table!
WILLEM:	I'm sorry.

Beat.

CASPER:	Though I admit you are not the only one with news.
BETSIE:	Papa!
CORRIE:	Papa, what are you hiding?
Casper:	We will have a new apprentice in the shop soon.
Corrie:	I hope you haven't promised to pay him much.
Casper:	A young man from out of town.
Willem:	Out of town?
Betsie:	Well where is he from?
CASPER:	From . . . Germany.
CORRIE:	What?
WILLEM:	Germany!?
BETSIE:	Papa, how can you?
CASPER:	Our Beje is open to any who knock! I will make no distinctions between German or Dutch or Jew--or anyone else.
	A young man needs lessons, and we will receive him. Who knows why a goose goes barefoot. Do you? We cannot know what good may come of it.

The group look around at one another in silence.

BETSIE: You're right, Papa. If he's one of these Nazis, then we'll receive him in kindness. Our hospitality shall be our protest. Isn't that right, Corrie.

CORRIE: I suppose so.

Silence for a beat.

BETSIE: Windowboxes!

CORRIE: What in the world are you on about, Betsie?

BETSIE: If we're to welcome a new guest, we must dress the windowboxes and see they are spilling over with flowers.

WILLEM: Flowers for Nazis? She's gone mad at last. Is it any wonder?

BETSIE: Nonsense. Windowboxes are a wonder. Come with me, Corrie. The market will be overflowing with tulips and we'll fetch the finest.

CORRIE: You go on. I've work to do in the shop. Papa will need my help.

BETSIE: Very well. But when this German arrives, he'll be greeted with windowboxes or I'm not Betsie ten Boom.

BETSIE exits.

CASPER: She is a wonder.

WILLEM: I'm off then.

CASPER: Give Tine and the children my love.

CORRIE: Goodbye, Willem.

WILLEM: Goodbye.

CORRIE: Come on, Papa. It's time to open.

CASPER: No time to waste.

SCENE 3

The Beje shop. CASPER *and* CORRIE *are at work.* OTTO *enters.*

OTTO:	Guten morgen.
CORRIE:	Hello. May I help you?
OTTO:	I am here to see Casper ten Boom. I have an appointment.
CASPER:	You must be Otto Schwarzhuber, come for the furtherance of knowledge and experience.
OTTO:	Yes, from Berlin. It seems a marvel that I should find much to learn in the nether reaches of Europe, but we shall see.
CASPER:	Perhaps you'll find more to appreciate here than you expect.
OTTO:	I doubt that. Is Herr ten Boom about, I prefer not to have my time wasted. I'd like to get right to work.
CORRIE:	This is Casper ten Boom, and we value manners here as well as good work.

OTTO: I apologize, fraulein. I expected someone . . . hmm . . . younger. I trust my workbench is prepared.

CASPER: Well, yes. Right over--

OTTO pushes his way behind the counter and looks around.

OTTO: Excellent. This will suffice. The first thing one learns in the Hitler Youth is efficiency. I will work as efficiently as possible and I expect my time to be treated likewise.

CORRIE: Well! I don't know what kind of efficiency you are used to in Berlin but in Haarlem you'll find courtesy is an efficacious quality in a young man.

BETSIE enters.

BETSIE: Isn't this lovely? How could anyone want to throw it out, Corrie? I found it in the alley outside.

BETSIE flourishes a rusty old teapot.

CORRIE: I'm not drinking anything out of that.

BETSIE: But it will make an irresistible flower pot. Just wait.

BETSIE removes flowers from a vase in the window and fills the teapot with them.

BETSIE: Oh! Hello, we haven't met. I'm Betsie. You must be Papa's new apprentice.

OTTO: Fraulein ten Boom.

Otto bows slightly. Betsie places the flower pot on his desk.

BETSIE: There you are. Do you like it?

CASPER: Otto was just telling us of the importance of his efficiency.

BETSIE: Really!? Oh, do tell.

OTTO: I wish to assume my duties and proceed with my work as soon as possible. Would you put this . . . elsewhere?

BETSIE: What do you mean?

OTTO: The desk, like the mind, functions best when uncluttered by that which is un-useful.

BETSIE: Un-useful? Well! If it's your position that flowers are useless then I suggest you've confounded your own argument by revealing the direst need for their "use."

OTTO: What?

BETSIE: Nevermind. I'll put them over here and you can "use" them whenever you find it's most efficient to do so.

CASPER: Let's stop wasting Otto's time and let him get to work. You may begin with this fine old Swiss piece from Mr. Kranz. It'll require a steady hand to repair. Let's test those skills of yours, eh?

Pickwick enters through the shop door.

CORRIE: Pickwick!

BETSIE: Pickwick!

PICKWICK: Ladies. Casper.

CORRIE: How lovely to see you.

PICKWICK: And, you, as always, Corrie. I wonder if I could have a word with your father?

CORRIE: If it's about your watch, he MUST approve the price with me before you leave.

Do you hear that, Papa?

PICKWICK: Not to worry. Only a short word.

BETSIE: I'll put on some tea.

BETSIE exits. PICKWICK and CASPER confer privately apart from the others. CORRIE stands at the end of the stage and listens from afar.

CASPER: How can I help?

PICKWICK: It's delicate, I'm afraid. Who's the stiff?

CASPER: A new apprentice.

PICKWICK: Can you trust him?

CASPER: I don't see why not. He's only just arrived, but I'm sure he'll work out.

What's this delicate business then?

PICKWICK: It's Jews.

CASPER: Jews? What about them?

PICKWICK: Willem came to see you, yes?

CASPER: He did.

PICKWICK: People are fleeing Germany by the hundreds, Casper. The thousands. And most of them are Jews.

CASPER: I've heard.

PICKWICK: There's a family at my home, but we haven't room to keep them. I'm sending them to Willem's home for the elderly.

CASPER: To Willem's?

PICKWICK: But they cannot go until the end of the week. Could they stay with you for a few days? Only a few.

CASPER: Well, yes, I suppose . . . but--

PICKWICK: But?

CASPER: Well. Otto. He's German.

PICKWICK: The stiff?

CASPER: Hitler Youth, I'm afraid.

PICKWICK: I thought you said you could trust him!

CASPER: Well, I only meant generally. I didn't know you were going to ask about Jews.

PICKWICK: Nevermind. It's no good, Casper. Do you think he heard?

CASPER: No, he's very diligent.

PICKWICK: I have to go. Forget what I've said. I'll find other arrangements.

The ticking of the great clock. Time slows. The scene freezes. Lt. Richter *enters. As* Pickwick *is frozen in his exit.*

Lt. Richter: A moment, please. This Mr. . . . Pickwick, was it? I don't have that name in my notes. Who is he?

Corrie: Pickwick? Only a friend. No one of any account.

Lt. Richter: And do you know what he and your father spoke about? Every detail could be important, Fraulein. Any little bit of information could be the key I need to help you and your family.

Corrie: Their business was that of the town, the people, who was in need, and who could be helped, and how. There's nothing criminal in that.

Lt. Richter: That remains to be seen. I do hope you are being honest with me. Are you sure there was nothing more?

Corrie: I'm sure.

Lt. Richter: Very well. Continue.

Lt. Richter *exits. The ticking of the clock fades. Time speeds along.*

SCENE 4

The lights come up on the Beje. Dinner. BETSIE, CASPER, *and* OTTO *enter.*

BETSIE: Careful. Careful.

BETSIE *carries food to the table.*

CORRIE: It smells wonderful, Betsie.

CASPER: Come. Come, Otto. You're our guest of honor. Sit.

OTTO: *(tentatively)*

        Thank you.

CASPER: Corrie, would you fetch it for me?

CORRIE *retrieves the family Bible from the shelf and hands it to* CASPER, *then sits as* CASPER *opens the Bible and reads.*

CASPER: Where were we, where were we . . . Ah, here.

        "We shall be delivered out of the hand of our enemies that we might serve him without fear in--"

OTTO: What is this?

CASPER: We read from Scripture before we eat dinner. A Ten Boom tradition. Right now we're in the book of--

OTTO: You'll have to excuse me.

BETSIE: Excuse you? Where are you going?

OTTO: I will not indulge the reading of that book of lies.

CORRIE: Book of what?!

OTTO: In Germany we have learned better than the keeping of fairy tales.

CORRIE: May I remind you that you are not IN Germany? In Holland we respect even those with whom we disagree. Perhaps Germany can do with a lesson in the efficacy of manners.

OTTO: I think the world will soon see what Germany can do.

BETSIE: Please. Sit, Otto. I want to hear all about Berlin.

CASPER: It's only a short passage and I'm sure it will not occupy your thoughts for long.

OTTO: Keep your tales to yourself. I am here to work, and that is what I will do. Good night.

OTTO exits.

CORRIE: How rude! How can you put up with this? You must fire him immediately, Papa!

CASPER: But he's an excellent worker. Why would I do that?

CORRIE: Why would you do that?!

The scene darkens. Time slows and the great clock ticks. As CORRIE *watches,* YOUNG CORRIE *enters crying, and sits on the stage with her face in her hands.* CORRIE *joins her, speaking in her place at times.*

CASPER: What's wrong, Corrie? What's happened?

CORRIE: The boys in the street, the ones from the market, they said I was ugly like an old milk cow and should stay in my barn.

CASPER: Did they now?

YOUNG CORRIE: I hate them.

CASPER: Hmm. I think they must not know what beauty is, or ugliness either, if they've said such a thing to my lovely daughter.

Wisdom tells the truth, you know. And they have not.

CORRIE: What do you mean?

CASPER: Look at me, Corrie. When we find something in the world that is wrong, we mustn't hate it. We must help it to become something different.

YOUNG CORRIE: But what if they weren't wrong. Maybe I am an ugly old milk cow.

CASPER: If that were the truth, then your papa would be a liar, wouldn't he?

YOUNG CORRIE: But . . .

CASPER: Listen. To see something rightly, you must see it with love, Corrie. Even if it only hates you in return. It's by loving that one becomes lovely. And that is why you are beautiful. Because I love you, and because you love me and Betsie and Willem and your mother.

See if you can love these boys, too. And then watch to see what will happen. Will you try?

YOUNG CORRIE nods, reluctantly.

CASPER: Now run along and help Betsie with her flowers.

YOUNG CORRIE exits. The ticking stops. Lights shift back to the Beje. Time speeds along.

BETSIE: Papa's right, Corrie. Think how wonderful Otto will be once he's learned to be polite. After that, there's no telling what we might make of him.

CORRIE: You're fools. Both of you.

CORRIE wanders downstage, out of the scene, and speaks to the audience, as if to LT. RICHTER.

CORRIE: We were, all of us, fools. He never should have been allowed to stay at all. What was papa thinking? He ought to have known.

LT. RICHTER enters.

LT. RICHTER: What exactly, ought he to have known? Fraulein?

CORRIE: Otto, of course. I could see it right away, but he was with us for months, his little cruelties and disrespect. I don't know how Papa and Betsie put up with him. Here was there until . . .

LT. RICHTER exits. The watch shop.

CASPER: Otto, have you repaired that movement I asked you about?

OTTO: Of course I did. I already told you.

CASPER: Ah, yes. Here it is, and good work too. In only two months, he's grown into a fine apprentice. Don't you think so, Corrie?

CORRIE: Shall I bill Mr. Janssen?

CASPER: Yes. It'll be ready to pick up this afternoon. Otto, would you fetch me that pinion on the counter?

OTTO rudely pushes past CASPER to fetch the tool. CASPER nearly falls.

CORRIE: Papa, are you all right?

CASPER: I'm fine. Lost my balance is all.

CORRIE: You nearly knocked him flat, Otto!

OTTO: The lot of the old is to make way for the young.

CORRIE: You will not speak that way of my father! You will show some respect--or you will leave!

CORRIE and OTTO stare one another down for a beat.

CASPER: Easy, Corrie. He meant no harm.

OTTO: Perhaps I should find other employment. My skills here are wasted on work that a child could do.

Otto goes back to his table as Willem enters.

CASPER: Willem!

WILLEM: Turn on the radio!

Betsie enters.

BETSIE: What's wrong?

Willem rushes to the radio and turns it on. Everyone gathers around it (except Otto) and listens. Otto packs his tools and edges toward the door.

WILLEM: The Prime Minister.

RADIO: " . . . we have secured for the Netherlands a place of neutrality. We will take no sides. We will, as always, remain a steadfast force for peace . . . "

Willem snaps the radio off.

CORRIE: But it's good news, Willem. Isn't it?

WILLEM: I trust no peace with Germany.

(Looking at Otto)

A darkness has been gathering. I fear it will soon sweep us into its shadow.

Otto exits.

BETSIE: Otto? Otto?

CASPER: He's gone.

BETSIE: Gone? Gone where?

CORRIE: Good riddance.

BETSIE: But will he be back?

CASPER: We did our best to teach him a trade, let us pray he will make good use of it in some other time and some other place.

CORRIE: Betsie would you take Papa and fix him some tea?

BETSIE exits with CASPER.

CORRIE: Do you really think there will be war?

WILLEM: Germany is a ticking time-bomb, Corrie, and it could explode at any moment. Papa knows this, though he tries to keep up appearances.

CORRIE: I'm afraid, Willem.

WILLEM: So am I. But I must get back to Tine and the children. Have faith, Corrie. We are hidden in the shadow of a mighty wing.

CORRIE and WILLEM exit. The lights darken. The clock ticks.

CASPER enters, looking around as though troubled in thought, followed by YOUNG CORRIE. CORRIE speaks for YOUNG CORRIE at times.

YOUNG CORRIE: Papa? Papa what's wrong?

CASPER: Nothing, Corrie. Only shadows in the night.

YOUNG CORRIE: What do you mean?

CASPER: Look there. Out the window. How far can you see?

CORRIE: It's too dark. I can see the street but only as far as Mr. Janssen's shop. Is something out there?

CASPER: Yes, dear. A great many things. They draw closer at every moment, while others recede into memory.

YOUNG CORRIE: You're scaring me, Papa. What's out there? Can it hurt us? What is it?

CASPER: It's the world, Corrie. The great, rolling epic of Creation. All around us, at all times, and in all places.

Beautiful things will happen. Terrible things will happen. But don't be afraid. Don't be afraid.

The clock ceases, CASPER and YOUNG CORRIE exit. The sounds of planes fill the Theater. Air raid sirens wail, and the thundering of far-off explosions fills the Theater. A flag of the Reich is unfurled over the stage.

A group of Jewish women enter.

JEWISH WOMAN: This way. Run!

GERMAN OFFICER: You there! Stop! Get them!

JEWISH WOMAN: What do you want?

The GERMAN OFFICER affixes yellow stars to the women.

GERMAN OFFICER: You will wear this so everyone can see what you are!

CORRIE, BETSIE, and CASPER enter, looking onto the street through the Beje window.

CORRIE: Are they Jews, Papa?

CASPER:	I fear they are.
	But pity the Germans as well, for they have touched the apple of God's eye.

The soldiers push the Jews off stage shouting at them as CASPER, CORRIE, and BETSIE look on.

BETSIE:	What do we do, Papa?
CASPER:	We pray. And we wait.
BETSIE:	Wait for what?
CASPER:	For our marching orders.

Light shift. The clock ticks. CASPER and BETSIE exit as LT. RICHTER ENTERS.

LT. RICHTER:	What exactly did your father mean by that? "Marching orders?" "The apple of God's eye?"
CORRIE:	The Jews are the people of God, they are close to his heart.
LT. RICHTER:	And this is why you hid them?
CORRIE:	I did not say that.
LT. RICHTER:	But it's true isn't it!?
CORRIE:	The truth is rarely so simple as we would like to believe, lieutenant.
LT. RICHTER:	And the truth is always most complicated for those who wish to evade it.
	So tell me, fraulein, why do you continue to evade it?

LT. RICHTER exits.

SCENE 5

The exterior of the Beje. THEA *enters stage left and looks around cautiously. She knocks on the Beje door.* CORRIE *and* CASPER *answer.*

CORRIE: Hello?

THEA: Please. Will you let me in? They will find me.

CORRIE: Who will find you?

THEA: Them.

The WOMAN *moves her scarf and exposes a yellow star.* CORRIE *pulls her inside.* BETSIE *enters.*

THEA: My name is Thea Dacosta.

CORRIE: How do you do, Thea? Won't you come into the kitchen?

BETSIE: I was about to make some tea, and you're just in time to join us.

CASPER: In this house, God's people are always welcome.

CORRIE: We have four empty beds upstairs.

BETSIE: Your only problem will be to choose which one to sleep in. But come. Give me a hand with the tea.

THEA follows BETSIE. As CORRIE hangs the coat, another knock.

CORRIE: Hello?

MEYER is at the door.

MEYER: I was told I might find a place to rest here?

CASPER: Well, yes, but . . . who told you . . .

MEYER presses past her into the Beje.

MEYER: Thank you, ma'am. I am a Jew, I must tell you. And God bless you. They've taken my family away and I dare not return to my own home.

CORRIE: My goodness. Come in. Come in.

Another knock. CASPER answers.

MARY: Thank you, dear. Am I in the right place?

CASPER: The right place?

MEYER: Yes, come in. Are you all right?

CORRIE: Is there anyone else, then?

BETSIE: I'll go make beds.

BETSIE draws MEYER and MARY into the kitchen to join THEA.

CORRIE: They can't stay here, can they? The Gestapo is just around the corner. They'll be found out in no time.

CASPER: We'll talk to Willem. Maybe he has room.

CORRIE: But who sent them?

CASPER: I don't know. But thank God we are able to help.

CORRIE: What in the world have we got ourselves into?

A sharp, commanding knock at the door. Everyone looks at one another and then CORRIE goes to answer.

PICKWICK: Miss Ten Boom? Open up. Quickly.

CORRIE: Pickwick?

CORRIE opens the door and PICKWICK enters.

CORRIE: What are you doing here? You're not a Jew are you?

PICKWICK: Hah! I should be so blessed. But come. I must talk with you all.

CORRIE and PICKWICK enter the shop and peek into the kitchen where the Jewish refugees are sitting. BETSIE joins them.

BETSIE: Pickwick! Is this your doing?

PICKWICK: I heard that Nazi of yours had fled and knew there was no one I trusted more than you, old friend.

CORRIE: But they can't stay here, Pickwick.

CASPER: The Gestapo station is only a block away!

CORRIE: It's a terrible idea.

BETSIE: It's a brilliant idea!

PICKWICK & BETSIE: They'll never think to look here!

CORRIE: But people come into the shop all the time.

PICKWICK: Ah-hah! If you're going to be part of the underground, you'll have to start out-thinking them.

CORRIE: The underground?

BETSIE: The underground?

Everyone grows silent as PICKWICK looks at each of them in turn.

CASPER: What must we do?

PICKWICK: I knew I could count on you Casper, and you too Betsie, and especially you Corrie.

CORRIE: Me?

PICKWICK: I've already spoken with Willem and he'll have room for them in a few days. We need your home as a step along the way. Willem will house people in the country while we find them transport to England or America or someplace safe.

But space isn't the problem.

CORRIE: I should think the Germans are the problem.

PICKWICK: Food is the problem. Ration cards. We can't feed people without ration cards, and we haven't found a means of counterfeiting them.

BETSIE: What do you suggest?

PICKWICK: Do any of you know anyone at the Food Office?

CORRIE: What about Fred?

CASPER: Of course!

PICKWICK: Who?

CORRIE: Fred Koornstra. He used to read the electric meter.

BETSIE: And I used to ask him in for tea, though he always refused.

CORRIE: I even taught his daughter when she was a young girl.

PICKWICK: Good. Good. And do you know his leanings?

CASPER: He's no Nazi, if that's what you mean.

PICKWICK: If he can help, you could ask him for, say, five ration cards . . . maybe ten? Shear them but don't skin them, as the saying goes. If we ask for too many it might raise suspicion.

Now, show me the house.

CORRIE: The house?

PICKWICK: Yes. I have an idea.

PICKWICK is given a tour.

BETSIE: My room is down there.

PICKWICK: Mmm. Hmm.

CORRIE: And Papa's is this way.

PICKWICK: Hmmm.

BETSIE: And this is Corrie's room.

PICKWICK: Ah hah.

CORRIE: Ah hah? What do you mean "Ah hah?"

PICKWICK: I will send someone in a few days. They will come with a delivery and give you the password--let's see, how about "Glockenspiel."

BETSIE: A password? Well this is exciting.

PICKWICK: Do as they say and they will take care of everything.

CORRIE: But what will they deliver?

PICKWICK: The less we say, the better. And from now on, my name will be Mr. Smit. And you will be Miss Smit. Everyone you meet in this work will be a Smit. The less we know one anothers' names, the better. Isn't that right, Miss Smit?

CORRIE: I suppose so . . . Mr. Smit.

PICKWICK: Goodbye for now. And thank you.

PICKWICK exits. The family looks at one another.

CASPER: Well then, you see? We have our marching orders.

They enter the kitchen where the refugees are gathered around the table.

CASPER: Welcome to the Beje.

CORRIE: We're so glad you're here. Let me get you a blanket.

BETSIE: Who would like some tea?

Light shift. LT. RICHTER enters.

CORRIE: We had guests at the Beje from time to time. But no one of any consequence. Father loved to invite, and Betsie loved to host. It was our way.

LT. RICHTER: I see. And these "guests," what were their names?

CORRIE speaks as the scene transitions.

CORRIE: Oh, so many! One so easily forgets in all the coming and going. We are busy people, Lieutenant. I'm sure you understand.

LT. RICHTER: I'm not sure I do. Help me to understand.

CORRIE: Well there was one guest that I remember in particular. It was, hmm, several years after the invasion . . . let me see . . .

SCENE 6

Soldiers pass to and fro on the street. CORRIE and PICKWICK confer in whispers, cautious of German eyes. A Jewish refugee is smuggled into the Beje and another is quickly smuggled out.

CORRIE crosses a name off of a list on a clipboard.

BETSIE: How many is that?

CORRIE: My goodness. That's a dozen already and we've only been in the underground for a week.

BETSIE: The war can't last long, I'm sure. But Pickwick is right. We're going to need food if there are any more.

Customers come and go from the Beje. WILLEM comes to retrieve another refugee. CORRIE crosses more names off her list. OTTO (now a Nazi officer) and SOLDIER 1 enter.

SOLDIER 1: Come on, what are you looking at?

OTTO: I used to work here.

SOLDIER 1: What? Here?

OTTO: It's been a long time, but I wonder ... I was an apprentice to an old watchmaker.

SOLDIER 1: Were they Jews?

OTTO: No, but almost as bad. They tried to read a Bible at me. Let's see if they're still here.

OTTO and SOLDIER 1 enter the shop.

CORRIE: Otto?

OTTO: Lieutenant Schwarzhuber.

CASPER: Why, Otto! You left so suddenly we didn't get to say goodbye. And look how you've grown!

OTTO: What do you think, Hans? Do we need a new watch? Shall we buy something?

SOLDIER 1: What have they got?

OTTO and SOLDIER 1 shoulder their way into the shop. SOLDIER 1 peruses the watches with OTTO as CORRIE slips into the kitchen.

CORRIE: Shh!

BETSIE: What's wrong?

CORRIE: It's Otto.

BETSIE: Otto? Oh dear. Stall him, Corrie.

CORRIE nods and goes back to the shop as BETSIE motions the Jewish refugees to hide.

CASPER: Are you looking for something in particular? Have you seen this fine piece? We only just put it on sale today.

OTTO: I doubt you've anything of much worth. I don't see Betsie, though, where is she?

CORRIE: Oh, you know, dishes, laundry, housekeeping. I could ask her to fetch some tea. Would you like some, Otto.

OTTO: Lieutenant Schwarzhuber. And yes. I am thirsty. I'll fetch it myself.

OTTO makes for the door to the kitchen but CORRIE steps in front of him.

CORRIE: She's in the middle of cleaning house and would be mortified if a guest saw it today. Betsie! Would you fetch some tea?

BETSIE: *(from the kitchen)*

Certainly, dear.

CASPER: Who's your friend, Otto?

OTTO: Lieutenant Schwarzhuber!

CASPER: Pleased to meet you, Lieutenant.

OTTO: Not him. Me. And I can get my own tea.

OTTO pushes past CORRIE into the kitchen where the Jewish refugees are hidden under the table, hidden from OTTO by the tablecloth. BETSIE is sitting, pouring tea. OTTO looks around suspiciously.

BETSIE: Otto!? It's been ages! Where on earth have you come from? And what are you wearing?

OTTO: It's Lieutenant Schwarz . . . nevermind.

BETSIE: I'll never forgive you for running off without saying goodbye. Here, have some tea.

Otto sips his tea and grimaces. He spits it back into the cup and puts it on the table.

BETSIE: Oh! Was it too weak? With the rationing we've taken to using the leaves several times. I'm afraid there's not much left to squeeze out of them.

OTTO: Disgusting.

BETSIE: Well now that's just rude, Otto.

Otto sees the Bible on the table and picks it up.

OTTO: Still reading this?

BETSIE: Always. It's a lantern in all manner of darkness.

OTTO: You're hiding something.

BETSIE: Hiding something? Whatever in the world do you think I'm hiding?

Do you mean the Jews under the table?

(beat)

OTTO: Don't take me for a fool.

BETSIE: I wouldn't dare, Otto. In fact, I take you for a smart young man in need of some . . . illumination.

OTTO: Illumination?

BETSIE: Yes, and if you're stationed here you should come by more often. You'll be warmer and safer in my kitchen than out on some battlefield.

OTTO:	My father is warden of a camp north of Berlin, did I ever tell you? He'll keep me off the front lines.
	I don't need anything from you.
BETSIE:	No. I'm sure you don't. But it's offered all the same. And when the day comes that you do need something of us, I hope we'll be able to provide it, whatever it may be. You have only to ask.
	You're always welcome here, Otto. Come and visit any time.

OTTO replaces the Bible and walks out.

OTTO:	Come on, Hans.
SOLDIER 1:	I thought we were going to buy . . .
OTTO:	There's nothing here worth my time.

OTTO exits, followed by SOLDIER 1. CORRIE runs into the kitchen.

CORRIE:	Is everyone all right? Did he see anything?
BETSIE:	Everyone's fine. But--
CORRIE:	We're going to need an alarm system.

The Jewish refugees crawl out from under the table.

MEYER:	That was a bold move, Miss ten Boom.
THEA:	You nearly gave me a good faint.
MEYER:	Easy now, Mary. Let me help you.
MARY:	Thank you, dear.

BETSIE: All's well now. And it was nice to see Otto again. Poor thing.

A knock at the door. CASPER answers. Two workman stand outside.

WORKMAN 1: I was told to see you about a glockenspiel.

CASPER: A glockenspiel?

WORKMAN 1: Yes, sir. A "glockenspiel."

CASPER: Why, yes. I think I can help with that. Come in.

The two men enter carrying a grandfather clock.

CORRIE: What's this?

CASPER: It's the "glockenspiel."

WORKMAN 1: And would you show us to Miss Smit's room?

The WORKMEN open the clock and remove masonry tools.

CORRIE: That is no proper way to treat so fine a clock.

WORKMAN 2: Can't be helped, I'm afraid. Have to smuggle it in so we don't catch the lingering eye of the Gestapo.

WORKMAN 1: We'll be done in no time.

CORRIE: Done? What are you going to do?

WORKMAN 1: Think nothing of it. You won't notice a thing.

WORKMAN 2: If we've done our job well, that is.

Just give us a few hours alone and we'll take care of everything.

CORRIE: Well, I suppose if Pickwick sent you . . .

WORKMAN 1:	You mean Mr. Smit?
CORRIE:	Yes, yes. Mr. Smit. This way.

CORRIE returns to the shop.

BETSIE:	Well? What are they doing? Did they deliver something?
CORRIE:	I'm not sure, but they don't want to be disturbed. In the meantime, we've got to have help feeding people if Pickwick is going to keep sending them. I'm going to see Fred Koornstra. I'll be back soon.
BETSIE:	Be careful, Corrie.
CASPER:	We don't know who we can trust.

CORRIE exits.

SCENE 7

CORRIE enters. The Food Office. She takes a deep breath and approaches MR. KOORNSTRA, who sits behind a desk.

MR. KOORNSTRA: Corrie!

CORRIE: Hello, Fred.

MR. KOORNSTRA: So good to see you. Is your father well?

CORRIE: He's well. Slower all the time, I'm afraid, but still ticking.

MR. KOORNSTRA: And what can I do for you? Is it about my daughter? She asks about you all the time, you know.

CORRIE: Oh, I do miss teaching her. I must come for a visit soon to see how she's doing.

MR. KOORNSTRA: She would be delighted. And we do love to have company.

CORRIE: That's just it, we've had some unexpected company at the Beje lately.

MR. KOORNSTRA: Unexpected company?

You haven't come about my daughter, have you?

CORRIE: First it was a single woman, then a man, and then . . . well the thing is, Fred . . . they are Jews.

MR. KOORNSTRA: I see.

CORRIE: But food is the trouble. They must eat. And they have no ration cards.

MR. KOORNSTRA: So you come to see me.

CORRIE: Fred, we've been friends a long time. Is there any way you can--

MR. KOORNSTRA: Those cards have to be accounted for a dozen ways, Corrie. They're checked and double-checked and--

CORRIE: Have you heard how the Germans are treating people like your daughter, Fred?

MR. KOORNSTRA: What do you mean?

CORRIE: The mentally disabled. Do you know what they do with them?

MR. KOORNSTRA: One hears rumors.

CORRIE: They round them up, Fred. They put them in camps. They "eliminate" them.

MR. KOORNSTRA: Yes. I know.

CORRIE: And that's what I'm hiding these people from, Fred. Do you understand?

Mr. Koornstra removes two ration cards from his coat and places them on the desk. Corrie considers them coldly.

Mr. Koornstra: I have these two left from last week. Please. Take them and go.

Corrie: Two, Fred? Listen to me.

Beat.

Corrie: What if ... what if there were a ... "hold up?"

Mr. Koornstra: *(paces in thought)*

A hold-up? Well. Yes. It might work. If it happened at noon when only my secretary and I are here ...

Corrie: ... and if they found you tied ...

Mr. Koornstra: ... and gagged! Yes, it could work ... and I know just the man who might do it! Do you remember Mr ...

Corrie: No! Don't! Don't tell me who! I don't want to know. Only get me the cards if you possibly can.

Mr. Koornstra: How many did you say you needed? Four? Five?

A beat.

Corrie: A hundred.

Mr. Koornstra: A hundred!?

Corrie: And that's for starters. It may be a long war, Fred.

MR. KOORNSTRA: Corrie, I don't know if--

CORRIE: I know you can do it, Fred. You must.

MR. KOORNSTRA: I will do what I can.

CORRIE: God bless you.

CORRIE exits.

SCENE 8

Corrie enters the Beje. Pickwick and Casper enter opposite.

PICKWICK: It's our finest work, I think.

CASPER: It seems rather small, doesn't it?

PICKWICK: Any bigger and it would attract attention.

Miss Smit!

CORRIE: Have your delivery men finished then?

PICKWICK: Come and see. Come and see.

Corrie, Casper, and Pickwick enter Corrie's bedroom, which has now had the hiding place added.

CORRIE: But it's smaller! What's happened?

PICKWICK: Yes, we've moved the wall. See?

CORRIE: But why?

PICKWICK: Show her, Mr. Smit.

Casper opens a secret panel. Corrie gasps.

PICKWICK: Go on. See for yourself.

Corrie climbs inside the hiding place.

PICKWICK: Next time there's trouble, get all your, shall we say, "watches" in here as quickly as you can.

CORRIE: It's so dark. They'll be terrified.

PICKWICK: Can't be helped.

BETSIE: We might put some water inside

CASPER: And a candle. Do you think?

PICKWICK: You must train them to be quick, and to be quiet. Once the alarm rings, it must take no more than sixty seconds for them to be hidden entirely. You must practice.

Corrie comes back into the room.

CORRIE: My goodness.

PICKWICK: This is dangerous work. Do you believe in it?

CASPER: I can think of no better work than that of making our home a refuge for those in need.

PICKWICK: No matter the cost?

CASPER: The cost? Hmm. Look at me, Pickwick. I am too old to fear the wrath of men.

My daughters will have to decide.

PICKWICK: Understand, my dears, that if you are caught, we can do nothing for you. I will deny I ever

	knew you. If the Germans snatch you up, prison, or worse, will be your fate.
BETSIE:	Christ stayed in the garden when he knew they would come. I will stay in my home and hope they do not.
PICKWICK:	What what about you?
CORRIE:	My place is here. I will keep watch. I will help however I am able.
PICKWICK:	Good.
	Any other questions?
CASPER:	God bless you and keep you, Pickwick.
PICKWICK:	Good bye, Mr. Smit.

PICKWICK exits.

BETSIE:	Well. We're certainly in the underground now.

Light shift. The ticking of the great clock. CASPER and BETSIE exit. CORRIE walks downstage. She reads from the Bible around her neck.

CORRIE:	"Do not worry beforehand how you will defend yourself. For I will give you words that none of your adversaries will be able to resist."

LT. RICHTER enters as CORRIE stows the bible in her shirt.

LT. RICHTER:	I am particularly interested in learning of your raids on the Food Office. Perhaps you can elaborate.
CORRIE:	There were no raids on the Food Office.

Lt. Richter:	Perhaps you call it something different. The matter at hand is how you came to be in possession of illegal ration cards.
	I am told your sister . . . Betsie was it? . . . has taken ill.
Corrie:	What? She's ill? Please let me see her. Is she all right?
Lt. Richter:	As I have told you. I am here to help. But you must help me first.
	So, the ration cards? Or the Jews perhaps. Which would you prefer?

Corrie walks downstage.

Corrie:	We stole no ration cards. We hid no Jews.

The ticking of the clock ceases. Light shift.

SCENE 9

Traffic in and out of the Beje. German patrols march past. CORRIE *and* BETSIE *keep lookout and motion Jewish refugees to enter and leave the house.* CORRIE *crosses names off her list.*

CORRIE: It's over a hundred now, Betsie!

BETSIE: And we've nothing left to eat but tulip bulbs. We need those ration cards, Corrie.

CORRIE: How can there be so many?

BETSIE: Have you heard any word from Fred?

A knock at the door.

CORRIE: Come inside, quickly.

META: Thank you!

CORRIE: Papa, we have a new "watch." Would you show her in.

CASPER: This way, dear. Willem will be by later to pick up the two "watches" from yesterday. Come, come. Follow me.

CASPER and META enter the kitchen. THEA and a JEWISH MAN and WOMAN enter and greet them.

THEA:	Hello!
CASPER:	This is Miss Thea Dacosta. Won't you tell us your name?
META:	Meta Montsano.
THEA:	Welcome, Meta. It's going to be all right now.
CASPER:	Thank you, Thea. Would you show her where we hide the "watches?"
THEA:	Certainly.
CASPER:	And let me get you some tea.

CASPER exits back to the shop, while THEA demonstrates the hiding place. The JEWISH MAN and WOMAN wait in the kitchen.

WILLEM arrives.

WILLEM:	Good morning, Corrie. Papa, said you have a couple of "watches" for me to deliver.
CORRIE:	Indeed I do. One moment.

CORRIE goes to the kitchen door.

CORRIE:	Come now. Quietly. Willem will see you safely out of the city.
WILLEM:	Hello. Stick with me and everything will be fine.
JEWISH MAN & WOMAN:	Thank you, sir!
WILLEM:	Take these papers. If anyone questions us, let me do the talking. Ready now? Wait. Wait.

A German patrol passes.

WILLEM: Now. Quickly. With me.

WILLEM and the JEWISH MAN and WOMAN exit. CORRIE crosses more names off her list. Germans are back and forth, checking papers. OTTO watches the shop from sidestage. MR. KOORNSTRA enters the shop. His face is bruised and beaten.

BETSIE: Fred!

CORRIE: Are you all right? Your face!

MR. KOORNSTRA: My friend took to his work with . . . rather more vigor than I expected.

BETSIE: Your friend?

MR. KOORNSTRA: *(smiling)*

Being robbed is no small adventure.

MR. KOORNSTRA opens his jacket and removes bundles and bundles of food ration cards.

CORRIE: Why, Fred, you've done it!

MR. KOORNSTRA: See they go to good use, Corrie. They cost only a bit of my pride this time, but if we are reckless, they could cost much, much more. Be careful. They are watching. They are always watching.

CORRIE: Thank you, Fred.

MR. KOORNSTRA: If you need more, I don't know what I can do, but I will help if I can.

CORRIE: You've done enough for now.

MR. KOORNSTRA: I must go before I'm missed.

MR. KOORNSTRA exits. CORRIE hides the ration cards under the stairs. BETSIE takes some cards.

BETSIE: We shall have a proper dinner tonight.

BETSIE exits. CORRIE hangs a closed sign on the shop window.

SCENE 10

The dinner table.

CASPER: Come. Come. Sit!

BETSIE: Dinner's almost ready, Papa. Don't rush!

CASPER: I'm not rushing anyone. Come. Come. Let me help you, Mary.

MARY: Thank you, Casper.

The Jewish refugees gather around the table and sit as CASPER *thumbs through the Bible looking for something to read.* CORRIE *and* BETSIE *set the table.*

MEYER: Do you know what I miss, Casper?

CASPER: If it's the kosher food, I'm sorry. There isn't much choice these days, I'm afraid.

MEYER: Music.

CASPER: Music?

MEYER: Before all this, my wife used to play piano after

	dinner. And when she did I'd dance with my daughter--even though she was just a tiny thing.
CORRIE:	How old was she?
MEYER:	My daughter? She'll be . . . nine now. I've missed two birthdays.
CORRIE:	What was it your wife used to play?
HENK:	Nothing German, I hope.
META:	Hear, hear.
MEYER:	What was it now . . . something by Chopin, I think.
HENK:	A Pole! Excellent. The Germans would have hated that.

MEYER *begins to hum Chopin's Waltz #3 in A-minor, Op. 34 no. 2. As he does so, the others join him.* MEYER *pulls* CORRIE *from her chair and dances with her. After a few moments everyone falls silent.*

CORRIE:	That was lovely. I'd forgotten how to do that.
MEYER:	We cannot forget. None of us.

Beat. MEYER *becomes emotional.*

CORRIE:	I'm sure they'll be all right, Meyer.

BETSIE *brings the final dish to the table.*

BETSIE:	Here we are.
CASPER:	I thought perhaps one of you might read for us tonight? One of the prophets, maybe? Or something from the Kethuvim? What do you think, Meyer?

MEYER: I would be honored.

MEYER puts on his yarmulke, flips through the Bible, and then begins to read. The Chopin waltz begins to play in the background.

MEYER: The elders of the daughter of Zion

Sit on the ground and keep silence;

The virgins of Jerusalem

Bow their heads to the ground.

As MEYER reads, Nazis patrol the streets. OTTO watches the Beje.

MEYER: My eyes fail with tears,

My heart is troubled;

Because of the destruction of the daughter of my people.

MEYER tries to continue, but cannot. CASPER finishes.

CASPER: How shall I console you?

To what shall I liken you,

O daughter of Jerusalem?

For your ruin is spread wide as the sea.

Who can heal you?

The music fades. OTTO exits.

CASPER: Thank you, Meyer. A hard reading, but well read.

BETSIE: Let's eat.

The group begins to eat. CORRIE and CASPER look at one another and nod. CORRIE gets up and walks to the shop. She rings the alarm. CASPER pulls out his watch and begins to monitor it.

CASPER: No time to waste! Go!

The group jumps into action. The table is cleared of all but three dishes. The chairs are pushed in, and the Jews run to the hiding place. When all is complete, CASPER shakes his head.

CASPER: Too slow. Too slow. We must be quicker!

CORRIE: It's all right. Only a drill. It's safe to come out.

Everyone returns to the table.

MEYER: I haven't had this much excitement since I was a boy.

THEA: I'm too old for excitement.

MEYER: Nonsense. A bit of excitement keeps one young. Isn't that right Miss Mary?

MARY: What?

THEA: Ignore him, Mary.

MEYER: I know what we need. We need a song to sing to keep us on pace. What do you think, Casper?

CASPER: A song?

MEYER: Come on, Henk. What's a good old tune?

HENK: Hava Nagila!

HENK and MEYER begin to dance and sing "Hava Nagila" while the others clap and laugh. The song finishes and everyone applauds.

BETSIE: Well then, NOW can we eat?

A knock at the door.

CORRIE: You go ahead. I'll get it.

CORRIE answers the door and PICKWICK enters the shop. Light shift. The scene at the dinner table is dimmed.

CORRIE: Good evening, "Mr. Smit."

PICKWICK: I can hear your "watches" ticking from a block away!

CORRIE: Oh my. Do you think anyone heard?

PICKWICK: Let us hope not. How are they?

CORRIE: Safe and sound, perhaps a bit stir crazy?

PICKWICK: You mean the Jews?

CORRIE: Well of course, I do. I feel like a revolving door, Pickwick!

(flipping through her clipboard)

> We've had . . . hundreds through the Beje since we began. And except for Meyer and Mary, you and Willem whisk them away so quickly we scarcely get to know their names. But they are such lovely people, all of them, Pickwick, I only wish . . .

PICKWICK takes the clipboard, tears the paper from the from it, shakes his head in disapproval and then wads it and puts it in his pocket.

CORRIE: But--what are you doing?

PICKWICK:	You are too free with your tongue, Corrie. That's what I've come to talk with you about.
CORRIE:	Now you have me worried. What is it?
PICKWICK:	They are onto us.
CORRIE:	What?
PICKWICK:	Someone is informing the Gestapo of our activities.
CORRIE:	Surely not!
PICKWICK:	A safehouse was raided last night. All the Jews have been arrested, as well as those who hid them.

Willem may be next. Or you. |
CORRIE:	But no, Pickwick. They can't. How . . .
PICKWICK:	We are almost certain we know who this man is. But we cannot arrest him. The Germans control everything.
CORRIE:	Well surely there is something we can do. Who is it?
PICKWICK:	Does it matter? The only question is what we are going to do about him.
CORRIE:	We've come this far, haven't we? What else must I do. I'm willing.
PICKWICK:	You don't yet know what I suggest.
CORRIE:	Out with it then.

PICKWICK: He would have to be . . . we could . . . kill him.

CORRIE: Kill him?

PICKWICK nods solemnly.

CORRIE: It's our goal to save life, Pickwick, not to destroy it.

PICKWICK: And what if by sparing this man's life, he destroys ours and others . . . theirs.

CORRIE: I don't know, Pickwick. I don't know the answer, but I cannot be party to murder. We cannot.

PICKWICK: I fear the consequences, Corrie.

But I agree.

Therefore we cannot be too careful. You must Guard your words at all times. If they come, if they suspect, they will question you, and you must answer with certainty. Do you understand?

CORRIE: I think so.

PICKWICK: Let us practice.

CORRIE: Practice?

PICKWICK: (slamming his hand on the table)

Where are you hiding your nine Jews?!

CORRIE: Nine? We only have five!

PICKWICK stands back and shakes his head.

CORRIE: I'm sorry. I have no facility with lying.

PICKWICK: Think of it not as lying, but as protection. You must be a shield that hides the lives in your keeping. Do you see?

If you're startled, anything may come out. You must be ready, Corrie. The Gestapo will try to trap you with words. Consider how you answer.

PICKWICK turns away, then spins and shouts again.

PICKWICK: The Jews you're hiding, where did they come from?

CORRIE: I . . . I don't know.

PICKWICK sighs.

CORRIE: Let me try again.

PICKWICK: You will have no second or third chances with the Gestapo. When they ask, there is but one answer. What is it?

CORRIE: What Jews? We have no Jews.

PICKWICK: Again.

CORRIE: What Jews? We don't have any Jews!

PICKWICK: AGAIN!

CORRIE: We don't have any Jews here!

PICKWICK: Where ARE they?!

CORRIE is shaken.

PICKWICK: Are you all right?

CORRIE: Yes. Yes, I'm fine.

PICKWICK: These are not games we play at, Corrie. The stakes are the very highest.

Now, look for Willem tomorrow night. He will come with further instructions and news from me.

You must pass on what I've said to your father and sister. I pray the day does not come, but if it should, God help us all.

PICKWICK exits.

CORRIE: We must keep up our practice.

CORRIE sounds the alarm and locks the door. Everyone jumps into action and exits, except for CASPER.

CASPER: What's wrong, Corrie. Was it Pickwick?

CORRIE: Nothing. It was nothing.

CASPER: You look like a ghost.

CORRIE: What are we doing, Papa? What will we do if they find out.

CASPER: We do what we are called to do. The rest is not our concern.

CORRIE: Aren't you afraid?

CASPER: Afraid? Of course, I am. But I wait for my ticket.

CORRIE: What?

CASPER: When you were a girl--only a little thing--do you remember when we would go in the summer to visit your Tante Jans in Amsterdam?

CORRIE: Tante Jans? What? No, I don't remember, Papa. It was a different world. What does that have to do with--

CASPER: We took the train. Think, Corrie. Do you remember how it was?

CORRIE: I . . . I remember you held my hand while we stood on the platform. And I remember the rumble of the train as it rolled into the station.

CASPER: Yes! It was all steam, and steel, and terror. You shook beside me and tried to pull away, but . . .

CORRIE: . . . I clung to you . . .

CASPER: . . . I and kept you.

CORRIE: It all seemed very big to me then. Terrible even. But I clung to your hand, and I knew I would be safe.

CASPER: And the ticket, Corrie? Think about the ticket. Do you remember?

CORRIE: I suppose we handed over our tickets and got onto the train. But what does it matter, Papa?

CASPER: I kept your ticket for you, and when the time came, I gave it to you just at the instant you needed it.

CORRIE: But if you hadn't given me the ticket, I couldn't have gotten on the train at all.

The great clock begins to tick. YOUNG CORRIE *enters and stands beside* CORRIE. *They speak in unison.*

Young Corrie: I don't understand.

Casper: You will. You will. My dear Cornelia Arnolda Johanna ten Boom. My little Corrie. When the hour comes for courage, your Father will give you everything you need, just at the moment you need it. With no time to waste.

Casper exits.

Young Corrie: Papa! Papa, don't leave me!

Young Corrie exits. The clock chimes once. It's nearly midnight on the great clock.

SCENE 11

Lt. Richter enters.

Lt. Richter: Our time here is nearly at an end. My patience thins.

Corrie: We kept no Jews. We conducted no raids.

Lt. Richter: Is that so.

Lt. Richter looks through his files.

Lt. Richter: You are a Christian, yes?

Corrie: I am.

Lt. Richter: Is there not a commandment that condemns those who bear false witness?

Corrie: There is but . . .

Lt. Richter: But you think yourself exempt from it?

Corrie: No. I . . .

Lt. Richter: The fact is, fraulein, you are no heroine

protecting the weak. You are no martyr who will be remembered.

What you are is simple. You are a liar.

Tell me, Fraulein ten Boom. What does God think of those who are liars, of those who steal, of those who hide secrets from the law? Has your God not set the authorities in their places? Does he not command you to obey those he has raised up?

CORRIE: We kept no Jews. We conducted no raids.

LT. RICHTER: Perhaps it would help if you considered me a priest. Consider this room your confessional. Tell me your sins, and I will absolve you. I will forgive you. The truth will set you free. Confess!

CORRIE: We kept no Jews. We conducted no raids. We kept no Jews. We conducted no raids.

LT. RICHTER: Do you know your father and sister have already confessed? Your brother is writing his own confession, even now. We know everything! You save no one with your lies. You protect nothing with your silence! Confess!

CORRIE: We kept no Jews. We conducted no raids.

We were watchkeepers. We kept our watches. We kept watch . . .

The ticking of the clock ceases. Light shift. LT. RICHTER *exits. Soldiers pass in front of the Beje.* WILLEM *enters and approaches the door. He knocks once before the Soldiers grab him from behind and drag him away. One of them removes* WILLEM's *coat and wears it as a disguise then gets to the door just as* CORRIE *answers.*

SOLDIER 1: Hello?

CORRIE answers the door.

CORRIE: We are closed.

SOLDIER 1: Your brother sent me.

CORRIE: Where is Willem? Why hasn't he come himself?

SOLDIER 1: He told me to come to you. My wife's been arrested. She's a Jew.

CORRIE: I told you, we are closed.

SOLDIER 1: There's a policeman who can be bribed for 600 guilders.

CORRIE: I think you have come to the wrong door. I don't see how I can help.

SOLDIER 1: If I don't get the money, she'll be taken away and it will be too late. Please. Your brother told me you were kind to her people.

CORRIE: Speak quietly! Come back in the morning. I will have the money.

SOLDIER 1: Thank you! I won't forget this.

CORRIE returns to bed. Outside, SOLDIER 1 backs away, removes WILLEM'S coat and puts his cap back on. OTTO and a GERMAN OFFICER approach along with SOLDIER 2. SOLDIER 1 nods and points at the house.

GERMAN OFFICER: Well done, Lieutenant Schwarzhuber.

OTTO: Thank you, sir.

GERMAN OFFICER: Get on with it then. If your intelligence pays off, there will be a promotion waiting for you.

Otto bangs on the door.

OTTO: Open! Open up!

Corrie bolts up in bed and Betsie sounds the alarm. The Beje erupts in action as the Jews run for the hiding place. Casper assists the Jews.

BETSIE: We're closed. Can you come back in the morning?

This old door sticks, I'm afraid.

OTTO: Open the door! Open it now!

CASPER: What's the meaning of this? It's the middle of the night!

Soldiers kick in the door and begin searching.

OTTO: Time is up, old man. Find them!

BETSIE: Otto, no. What have you done?

OTTO: Sit!

Just as the soldiers reach Corrie's room, the Jews are in the hiding place.

GERMAN OFFICER: Seize her! Where are they?

CORRIE: What?

GERMAN OFFICER: Jews. Where are you hiding them?

CORRIE: I don't know what you're talking about.

GERMAN OFFICER: Give me your papers. Now!

Corrie hands him papers. The German Officer tears them in half.

GERMAN OFFICER: Where are the Jews!

CORRIE: I told you. I don't know anything about . . .

The OFFICER strikes her. Behind the bedroom wall, the Jews cower in terror as CORRIE is questioned inches away.

GERMAN OFFICER: Tell me!

CORRIE: What Jews? We have no . . .

GERMAN OFFICER: Where are the ration cards!

The OFFICER presses her against the wall.

Corrie: I don't know. We don't have any . . .

GERMAN OFFICER: You have stolen ration cards. You have offered to make bribes. And you are hiding Jews in a secret room in this house! Where are they!

The OFFICER slams her against the wall of the hiding place.

CORRIE: Jesus, protect me.

GERMAN OFFICER: Say that name again and I will kill you.

The GERMAN OFFICER lets CORRIE loose and she slumps to the floor.

GERMAN OFFICER: If you won't talk, the other one will. Let's go!

The OFFICER pushes her into the shop. CASPER and BETSIE are held at gunpoint in chairs.

GERMAN OFFICER: Sit!

OTTO: She'll be the ringleader.

GERMAN OFFICER: Take that one and make her talk.

A SOLDIER hustles BETSIE offstage.

CORRIE: Betsie!

CASPER: Let her be!

GERMAN OFFICER: She'll be fine if she tells the truth.

CASPER: We are law-abiding citizens.

GERMAN OFFICER: *(snatching the Bible from the table)*

Law-abiding? What does your book, say about obeying the government?

CASPER: Fear God, and honor the king . . . or queen in our case.

The GERMAN OFFICER spits and throws the book on the ground.

GERMAN OFFICER: FIND THEM!

The GERMAN OFFICER overturns the table.

SOLDIER 1: We've looked everywhere, sir. If they're here, the devil himself has hidden them.

The SOLDIER returns with Betsie, whose lip is bleeding.

SOLDIER 2: The same from this one. She won't talk.

GERMAN OFFICER: Get them out of my sight. Set a watch in the house and starve the Jews where they hide.

CORRIE: There's no one here!

GERMAN OFFICER: I'll give you one last chance, old man. Tell us where they are and you can live out your days in peace. The truth is your ticket to freedom.

CASPER looks at CORRIE and BETSIE and smiles at them and stands to face the OFFICER.

CASPER: If you free me today, tomorrow my house will be open to any who knock.

GERMAN OFFICER: Take them!

Soldiers seize CASPER and BETSIE.

CORRIE: Papa! Where are you taking him?

BETSIE: Papa! No!

GERMAN OFFICER: We've prisons hungry for this kind of filth.

BETSIE is dragged offstage in the opposite direction of CASPER, leaving CORRIE alone centerstage.

CORRIE: Betsie! Where are you taking her?

BETSIE: Corrie!

GERMAN OFFICER: No one comes in. No one goes out. We'll turn these Jews to mummies.

Light shift. The great clock ticks as the GERMAN OFFICER exits. LT. RICHTER enters, stepping around the overturned table.

CORRIE: We kept no Jews. We conducted no raids. We kept watch.

LT. RICHTER: Then perhaps you are beyond my help, Fraulein ten Boom. A pity.

The ticking ceases.

Beat.

CORRIE: May I tell you the truth, Lieutenant?

LT. RICHTER: This entire meeting is predicated on the assumption that you will do exactly that.

CORRIE: We Dutch have a saying: "There is more in it than an empty herring."

There is more than meets the eye.

You and I have eyes only for the empty herring, but God's perspective is infinitely higher.

In his eyes, the poorest among us, the weakest, those whom the powerful do not see and will not value, are worth more than we can imagine, even more than a watchmaker--or a lieutenant.

LT. RICHTER considers CORRIE coldly as he removes a letter from his pocket.

LT. RICHTER: Do you see this? It is a letter. For you. Would you like me to read it?

CORRIE: A letter? From who?

LT. RICHTER: From Tine ten Boom, your brother's wife, I believe.

CORRIE: What does it say? I've had no news.

LT. RICHTER: She says:

(reading)

"Corrie, can you be very brave."

CORRIE: What? Why? What does she say?

A startling, brilliant light shines from upstage.

LT. RICHTER: "I have news that is hard to write."

CASPER enters and walks past CORRIE into the light as LT. RICHTER reads.

CORRIE: Oh no. Oh, God.

LT. RICHTER: "Your watches are safe. But Papa survived his arrest . . . by only ten days. He is now with God."

The light vanishes and CORRIE falls to the floor and cries.

LT. RICHTER: Your "papa" died alone in an empty hall, not far from this room. I watched him die, and his body was tossed into an unmarked grave. Tell me: What kind of god would allow that?

Like the Jews, you cling to tales of a god who continually demonstrates his contempt for you. But look around, fraulein. Where is he now? Will he save you? No. He will leave you alone . . . to die, like he did your father.

CORRIE: You don't understand. The watches are safe. Praise God.

LT. RICHTER: No, Fraulein ten Boom, it is you who do not understand. And before the end, you will see much more of what god is willing to allow. Your feeble praises will dry in your throat. You will be swept aside with the rest.

Goodbye, fraulein.

Where you are going now, you will find that help is a dream from which you are about to sharply awaken. Auf Wiedersehen.

LT. RICHTER exits. The set is rolled away leaving CORRIE in a vast open darkness.

Betsie is dragged onstage by a Soldier.

CORRIE: Betsie! Are you all right?

BETSIE: Corrie, thank God.

SOLDIER 2: Prisoners are not to speak!

A train whistle wails. A crowd of emaciated women enter.

SOLDIER 1: Make room! Get back.

SOLDIER 2: Hurry up! Get aboard!

The Soldiers herd Corrie and Betsie as into a train car.

CORRIE: Where are they taking us?

BETSIE: I don't know. Stay with me.

Corrie pulls out the bible from around her neck and clutches it, kisses it.

BETSIE: What is this? You have a bible. Here? Don't let them see. Hide it, Corrie. Hide it.

CORRIE: Papa's dead, Betsie. He's gone.

BETSIE: He's not gone, Corrie. He's been released.

CORRIE: What?

BETSIE: He's robed in glory now. Papa won't have to suffer like us.

Corrie weeps and stashes her bible. The great clock begins to tick.

BETSIE: Hush. Save your tears. We'll be in Germany soon.

Corrie & Betsie vanish into darkness as the train pulls away. Young Corrie enters, lost.

YOUNG CORRIE: Papa? Papa, where are you? Don't leave without me. Don't leave me alone.

YOUNG CORRIE exits into darkness. The clock tolls midnight with a thunderous chime. The refugees in the Hiding Place cower and quiet one another as the clock chimes.

MEYER: Hush.

THEA: Listen.

Curtain.

ACT 2

SCENE 1

The clock ticks a few moments and then suddenly stops. CORRIE *enters and looks around.*

CORRIE: I'm still here, in the silences between moments . . . listening. I hear the tick, it follows the tock, and so on, and so on, counting away the hours, the days, the years, as if to say . . . what?

I can nearly make it out . . . in Betsie's voice sometimes--

BETSIE: *(offstage)*

"You have only to ask . . . "

CORRIE: --and so often in Papa's. It sounds like . . .

CASPER: " . . . some other time, and some other place . . . "

CORRIE: I'm listening but . . .

The ticking of the great clock. CASPER *is at work at his bench in the Beje shop. As he works, the clock ticks irregularly until at last the ticking is normal.* CORRIE *watching, speaking at times instead of* YOUNG CORRIE.

CASPER: Ah, there we are. Right on time.

YOUNG CORRIE and YOUNG BETSIE enter.

YOUNG CORRIE: What are you doing, Papa?

CASPER: What am I doing? Exactly what I'm meant to do, of course. I'm fixing Mister DeVries pocketwatch.

YOUNG BETSIE: Can we help you?

CASPER: You are already helping me.

YOUNG CORRIE: We are?

CASPER: Naturally, you remind me that the work of watches is not nearly so important as the work of daughters.

CORRIE: Am I work?

CASPER: Well, yes. And no. You're not work like fixing a watch, but you are work like that of a great artist. Do you know that our Father says we are his poems?

YOUNG BETSIE: I'm a poem?

CASPER: You are, and one of my favorites. You too, Corrie.

YOUNG CORRIE: I don't feel like a poem.

CASPER: No, I suppose you don't, but in a poem each and every word is placed just so, no more and no less than are necessary for its exact meaning.

CORRIE: But what do I say? What do I mean?

CASPER:	It takes us a lifetime to understand what we mean. So we must look, and we must listen to our lives at all times.
YOUNG BETSIE:	Because beautiful and terrible things will happen?
CASPER:	Mmm hmm. That's true.
YOUNG CORRIE:	But why? I don't want anything terrible to happen.
CASPER:	There's my little philosopher. Asking questions bigger than both of us. You're trying to carry my suitcase again.

Beat.

CASPER:	I don't know why, Corrie. But perhaps it's through suffering we get into glory . . .

The ticking of the great clock resumes. The Theater goes entirely dark, YOUNG CORRIE and CASPER exit.

CASPER:	*(offstage)*
	. . . perhaps it's through darkness that we get into the light.

A powerful beam of light shoots across the stage.

YOUNG CORRIE & CORRIE:	*(offstage)*
	Papa? Betsie! Don't leave me!

The ticking clock gives way to the deafening sound of a train whistle. YOUNG CORRIE exits. The light is assumed to be that of the train engine thundering through the night. The train car enters with its prisoners.

JESKE: Give her room!

TRUDKA: Be quiet!

JESKE: Stay with me, Avien.

BETSIE: *(coughing)*

Is there any water?

TRUDKA: Water? Hah! Did you think you had a first class ticket?

CORRIE: She's not feeling well.

TRUDKA: She's no worse off than the rest of us.

CORRIE: Do you know where they're taking us?

TRUDKA: How would I know?

JESKE: I think there's a dead woman over there.

TRUDKA: There are two dead in the corner, that I saw. They're better off.

TRUDKA and another prisoner begin to fight.

PRISONER 1: I can't breathe! Give me room.

TRUDKA: Get off me!

PRISONER 1: I can't... I can't...

JESKE: Someone help her!

TRUDKA: Keep her away from me.

PRISONER 1 faints and slips to the floor.

The women cry, groan, scream, push, shove, and grope with one another until the train comes to rest. They exit the car. The train exits and they find themselves before the gates of Ravensbruck. Guards enter shouting and threatening the prisoners.

GUARD 2:   In line! Ranks of five! Stand up! Get in line!

GUARD 1:   Get that old one off the ground.

JESKE: Please, she can't stand. Her legs . . .

GUARD 2:   Get her out of here.

The PRISONER 1 is dragged offstage to the right and shot while everyone else is herded off to the left. The women scream offstage. THE BEAST enters the bare stage, holstering her pistol, and appraises the audience.

THE BEAST: Welcome to Ravensbruck. Here you will find everything you require. I will provide it. Beds. Food. Work. If you follow my rules, you will keep these things, and you will live. If you do not obey or you cannot work, you will lose what you require, and what becomes of you is not my concern.

            Do you understand?

Silence.

THE BEAST: Do you understand?

Offstage, the prisoners answer.

THE BEAST: Good. Inform the prisoners of the function of the bunkers--and the pole.

GUARD 2 enters.

GUARD 2:   The bunkers are for those who fail to cooperate.

The GUARD opens a door the size of a gym locker, revealing GITA crammed into the space and hung from her hands. The GUARD hauls her out and GITA collapses.

THE BEAST: Get her up.

GUARD 2: UP! Do you want to go back inside!

GITA tries to rise but falls.

GITA: No. No, please.

THE BEAST: Stand up.

GUARD 2: UP!

GITA climbs to her feet. The GUARD approaches the pole, bloody shackles hang from it.

GUARD 2: And the pole? The pole exists for one reason: to cleanse the mind of illusion. Its instruction is efficient--and painful. Pray you do not require its lesson.

THE BEAST: Arbeit Macht Frei. Work will set you free. Not an escape. Not an invasion of Americans or Soviets. Work. You must save yourself. Do think you can do that?

GITA: Yes, ma'am.

THE BEAST: Good. Any questions?

GITA: No, ma'am.

THE BEAST: Bring me the new ones.

CORRIE, BETSIE, JESKE, AVIEN, and TRUDKA are paraded onto the stage by GUARD 2 and line up in front of THE BEAST. AVIEN clings to her mother, JESKE.

| GUARD 2: | Line up! Single file! Move. No touching! |

THE GUARD forces JESKE and AVIEN apart.

JESKE:	Please, she's my daughter!
GUARD 2:	No talking!
AVIEN:	Mama!

JESKE breaks the line and tries to hold AVIEN.

| THE BEAST: | Bring her to me. |

THE GUARD pushes AVIEN toward the THE BEAST.

| JESKE: | No! |
| THE BEAST: | I will give you what you need, child. Do you understand? No one else. Only me. |

AVIEN nods in terror.

| JESKE: | No, please! Avien! |

THE BEAST nods at the GUARD who drags JESKE to the bunker.

THE BEAST:	*(to Avien)*
	Now, get in line, child. I will not ask again.
	Get them cleaned and inspected with the rest. They will be assigned work details in the morning.

THE BEAST exits. The Guards and prisoners enter. Guards put them through a process in which they are given prison clothes, inspected, and accounted for.

| GUARD 2: | Move! |

CORRIE: That dear girl, in the bunker...

Come here, child.

CORRIE comforts AVIEN.

BETSIE: The Guard, Corrie. That poor creature.

CORRIE: The Guard?

BETSIE: The pain she must carry, to have such hatred inside of her. It must be awful.

CORRIE: You're talking foolishness. It'll be all right, Avien.

AVIEN: I want my mama.

CORRIE: Hush. Hush now. Stay with me.

BETSIE: If the Germans can learn such hate, think how they could be taught to love.

CORRIE: What?

GUARD 2: Move!

GUARD 1: Get in line for inspection. Strip!

Prisoners are herded off the stage. CORRIE remains in the center. The great clock ticks. As she speaks, she slowly disrobes, but beneath her clothing is a prison uniform.

CORRIE: Our shoes. Our clothes. Our jewelry.

TRUDKA: *(offstage)*

No! That was my mother's!

CORRIE: Her watch. Her glasses. Rings. Single, lonely wedding rings in piles on a table. Betsie's necklace and our papers and "Old Blue," our passports, all the things that told us who we were. The . . . even the gold fillings in our teeth.

Offstage a prisoner yells in pain.

CORRIE: And what did we have left? What else could they take?

(as she removes her shirt)

Dignity. Humanity. Hope.

They took everything from us.

Offstage, weeping.

BETSIE: *(offstage)*

Not everything.

CORRIE remembers something. She pulls the bible out of her blouse. It still hangs around her neck.

CORRIE: No. Not everything. By grace, one thing remained . . . hidden.

BETSIE enters in her prison garb.

CORRIE: Look!

CORRIE shows BETSIE the Bible.

BETSIE: A lantern in the dark.

Other prisoners are herded onstage in prison robes.

BETSIE: Quick, they're coming!

Transition to the barracks.

GUARD 2: Forward. Move.

GUARD 1: There will be a roll call in the morning and you will all be assigned to work.

GUARD 2: Inside, all of you.

The prisoners are herded into a building filled with bunks. The Guards do not enter but stop at the doorway. The women crowd into the beds, piling on top of one another and fighting for room.

CORRIE: Ouch!

TRUDKA: Let me in!

CORRIE: Up here with me, Avien.

AVIEN: Where's my mama?

CORRIE: She'll be here soon. Hush now.

BETSIE: There's room here.

GITA: Ouch!

TRUDKA: What's that?

CORRIE: Something's biting me!

GITA: Fleas!

TRUDKA: They can't expect us to sleep here.

CORRIE: Fleas, Betsie! The beds are crawling with them!

BETSIE: We should be grateful.

CORRIE: Grateful? For fleas?

BETSIE: For a bed, at least. And yes, maybe fleas as well.

TRUDKA:	They'll get no thanks from me. Ouch!
GUARD 1:	Lights out!

The lights drop.

BETSIE:	Goodnight, Corrie.
CORRIE:	Goodnight.
BETSIE:	Lord, bless us and keep us.
GITA:	I don't have room! Move over.
BETSIE:	Lord lift up your face to shine upon us . . .
CORRIE:	Go to sleep, Betsie.
BETSIE:	. . . and give us peace.
TRUDKA:	Move over!
BETSIE:	Amen.

SCENE 2

A bell rings. The lights come on.

GUARD 2: Roll call! Get in formation!

THE BEAST: Ranks of five!

The prisoners begin to sound off by number. JESKE is dragged from the bunker. She stumbles into the line. AVIEN runs into her arms.

GITA: Are you all right?

GUARD 2: No talking! No touching! Sound off!

All prisoners sound off (add additional numbers if required by staging).

GITA: 45764

TRUDKA: 52392

(whispering)

Chin up, Jeske. Play their game . . . sound off.

JESKE: 62344

CORRIE: 66730

BETSIE: 66729

Silence.

THE BEAST: Where is prisoner 64521?

The prisoners look around in confusion.

GUARD 2:   64521 is dead. That's 37 dead this morning.

THE BEAST: Split them up and get them to work.

The Guards move among the prisoners dividing them.

THE BEAST: Send those to the knitter's brigade. The rest to Siemens.

BETSIE *is sent to knit and exits.* CORRIE *is sent to the Siemens factory.*

Corrie's group is herded into the factory and sits before a table. MOORMAN *passes out radio parts and welcomes them. A* GERMAN OVERSEER *enters.*

MOORMAN: Good morning, sir.

GERMAN OVERSEER: We continue to receive complaints of defective wiring. Quality control must improve.

MOORMAN: Yes sir.

GERMAN OVERSEER: These new workers should help. That one was a watchmaker, I'm told. Perhaps you will find some use for her.

MOORMAN: A watchmaker?

The GERMAN OVERSEER *exits while the prisoners begin work.*

MOORMAN: Is it true?

CORRIE: I make watches, yes. In my father's shop. In Haarlem.

MOORMAN: You're the first woman I've met who is trained in technical work. How wonderful. You may enjoy what we do here.

CORRIE: And what is that precisely?

MOORMAN: Radios. For airplanes. Can you solder?

CORRIE: Of course I can.

MOORMAN: Then look here. Make it like this. Do you see?

CORRIE: Perfectly.

The prisoners work at assembling radios.

MALE PRISONER GREEN 1: Where are you from?

CORRIE: Haarlem. In Holland.

MALE PRISONER GREEN 2: Holland, eh? We had another Dutch. They took him away last week.

MALE PRISONER GREEN 1: Haven't seen him since.

MALE PRISONER GREEN 2: I'm from Prague. He's from Leipzig.

CORRIE: Why did they send you here?

PRISONER RED: *(laughs and points at his patch)*

They didn't tell you about the patches?

Corrie: *(considering hers)*

No.

FEMALE PRISONER BLACK: A red triangle, like yours, is for political. He's a red too. Gave a speech on a street corner, and now he's stuck here.

CORRIE: What about hers?

PRISONER RED: Hah! The lavender for the pacifist. Jehovah's Witnesses.

CORRIE: And what about her, what's black?

MALE PRISONER GREEN 2: Prostitute, gypsy, addict, what does it matter. By the looks of her, she's one of those Rhinelanders. Stay away from her.

FEMALE PRISONER BLACK: Really, you give such compliments! I'm flattered. It's those greens you have to watch out for. Criminals every one. Thieves, murderers.

MALE PRISONER GREEN 2: Are you trying to sweet talk me?

FEMALE PRISONER BLACK: You should be so lucky.

CORRIE: And yellow. For Jews, I suppose?

PRISONER RED: They have it the worst.

MALE PRISONER GREEN 1: Not many left.

PRISONER RED: They don't last long.

FEMALE PRISONER BLACK: They ship them off to Auschwitz.

MALE PRISONER GREEN 2: God knows what becomes of them there.

JEWISH PRISONER: You know we can hear you over here?

The GERMAN OVERSEER returns.

GERMAN OVERSEER: *(inspecting a radio)*

    Yes, these will do.

MOORMAN: Thank you, sir.

GERMAN OVERSEER: When I return I expect them to be on quota.

MOORMAN: Yes, sir.

MOORMAN inspects Corrie's work.

MOORMAN: My dear watch-woman! Excellent work! But this will not do!

CORRIE: What? But I've done it perfectly!

MOORMAN: Have you forgotten who you are working for? These are radios for fighter planes!

MOORMAN pulls wires out of her radio.

CORRIE: What did you do that for?

MOORMAN: Now. Solder them back wrong. And you are already over your quota. You must slow down.

PRISONER RED: Like this.

MOORMAN: Slow and easy does it. Watch, and you will learn, watch-woman.

MALE PRISONER GREEN 1: Even in here, we may fight.

JEWISH PRISONER: The quality of our work shall be our protest.

CORRIE: Won't someone notice if the radios don't work?

MOORMAN: That is not our concern. Ours is to resist. The rest is up to God.

MALE PRISONER GREEN 1: Shall we?

The prisoners begin redoing the work they've just done.

MOORMAN: Well done. Load up.

PRISONER RED: *(to Corrie)*

This way.

The prisoners pick up boxes of completed radios and haul them offstage.

SCENE 3

The barracks. BETSIE is in the bed. CORRIE enters.

CORRIE: Betsie!

BETSIE: *(coughing)*

There you are.

CORRIE: Where did they take you?

BETSIE: Socks. Whole legions of us.

CORRIE: Socks?

BETSIE: Isn't it funny. We sew socks. But I must tell you something awful.

CORRIE: What is it?

BETSIE: We make the heels too thin. The poor boys who wear them will get little comfort, I'm afraid. What about you?

CORRIE: The same. But radios.

BETSIE:	Radios? Well that sounds much more interesting than socks.
CORRIE:	None of them work. I daresay someone's bound to find out and I hope I'm not there when they do.
BETSIE:	Will you help me sit up? Do you still have your Bible?
CORRIE:	Yes. It's right here.
BETSIE:	I miss Papa reading before dinner.
CORRIE:	So do I.
	I wonder if Willem and Tine are all right, and the children. Surely Pickwick will have got out safe.
BETSIE:	Pickwick? He's too smart for them, I think.
CORRIE:	I hope you're right. I wish Papa was here.

Beat.

BETSIE:	Do you think you could be a martyr, Corrie?
CORRIE:	What?
BETSIE:	Like Papa.
CORRIE:	Like Papa? He'd never call himself a martyr.
BETSIE:	Isn't he though?
CORRIE:	Well, it's not how I ever imagined such a thing, but maybe you're right.
BETSIE:	I think maybe I could.

CORRIE: Could what?

BETSIE: Be a martyr.

CORRIE: That's awful, Betsie, don't talk like that.

BETSIE: But they'd have to kill me quick or I'd lose my nerve.

CORRIE: No one's getting killed. What's all this morbid talk? It isn't proper and you know it.

BETSIE: You're right, of course. Let me see it, Corrie. Now that Papa's gone, I'll read for us.

BETSIE takes the Bible and goes to the table. She reads quietly as CORRIE crawls into bed and the other prisoners enter.

BETSIE: "For whoever wishes to save his life will lose it; but whoever loses his life for My sake will find it."

GITA: What's that?

TRUDKA: They don't allow books.

CORRIE: Let her be. She needs rest.

BETSIE: Shall I read it to you?

TRUDKA: *(looking around)*

To who? Me?

BETSIE: To whomever will listen.

BETSIE begins to read and as she does so, prisoners quiet and gather around.

BETSIE: "My bones grow old, for day and night Your

> hand is heavy upon me;
>
> My vitality turns into the drought of summer.
>
> But You are my hiding place;
>
> You shall preserve me from trouble;
>
> You shall surround me with songs of deliverance."

JESKE: Keep reading.

GITA: What is it?

BETSIE: What is it? It's from the Psalms.

GITA: What's a psalm?

BETSIE: Well, it's like a song, written a very long time ago.

TRUDKA: My mother took us to church, but my father always told us it was nonsense.

BETSIE: Would you like to hear another?

JESKE: Yes, please.

BETSIE: "Strengthen the feeble hands, steady the knees that give way;

> say to those with fearful hearts,
>
> 'Be strong, do not fear;
>
> your God will come.'"

JESKE: I like that.

GITA: What's it about?

TRUDKA: My father was right.

GITA: What do you mean?

TRUDKA: It's about Jews. And if being saved means being treated like a Jew, I'll pass. I'd rather be here than Auschwitz.

JESKE: Why? What happens at Auschwitz?

TRUDKA: Never you mind. Just see you don't get sent there.

JESKE: What do you think, Tante Betsie? What does it mean?

TRUDKA: Go on. Tell her. Tell her how your God is saving us all.

CORRIE: Leave her alone.

TRUDKA: Don't count on it. Any of you. The only way out of here is up that smokestack or on a train to Poland.

JESKE: What do you say?

BETSIE: Well. It's mystery isn't it?

TRUDKA: It's just an old story.

JESKE: What kind of a mystery?

BETSIE: The kind that's a promise. A promise that the lightning crack of justice has already struck, and we live in the silence before the thunderclap.

On a quiet night, like this one, if you listen carefully, you may hear the distant rumble of its approach.

Silence is kept.

TRUDKA: I told you she was crazy.

JESKE: Thank you, Tante Betsie.

GUARD 1: LIGHTS OUT! No talking!

The Prisoners scramble for space on the beds.

CORRIE: You sound like Papa.

BETSIE: We have to teach them, Corrie. Maybe that's why we're here.

CORRIE: We're here because they caught us. Go to sleep. You need your rest.

GITA: Will you read to us again tomorrow.

BETSIE: Of course I will, dear. Of course I will.

The lights go out. CORRIE *steps to the edge of the stage.*

CORRIE: Days into weeks into months. Work, sleep, line up, work, sleep, line up. Like a wheeling machine, the camp ground our bones to dust. And as we listened, we heard only the approach of a harrowing silence. A silence that swallows the voice, that quenches color, that serves only the filling of its own belly.

Work, sleep, line up. Work sleep, line up, work, sleep . . .

SCENE 4

Guards enter.

GUARD 1: Get out! Roll call!

GUARD 2: Move, swine! Line up for inspection.

BETSIE is sick and requires assistance getting out of bed.

GUARD 2: Get OUT here! What's wrong with that one?

CORRIE: Please, she's unwell.

THE BEAST: Get her in line.

OTTO enters.

THE BEAST: Good morning, sir.

OTTO: Are they ready for inspection?

THE BEAST: Yes, captain. All prisoners reporting.

OTTO walks slowly down the ranks and inspects the prisoners.

OTTO: This one is too old.

A GUARD pulls the PRISONER out of the formation and escorts her away.

OTTO: And what have we here?

THE BEAST: Prisoner 66729.

OTTO: Look at me "66729."

BETSIE looks at OTTO.

BETSIE: Otto? Is that you?

THE BEAST: Prisoners are NOT to speak!

THE BEAST moves to hit BETSIE.

CORRIE: No!

OTTO raises his hand to stop THE BEAST.

OTTO: I told you, didn't I?

CORRIE: Told me? What did you tell me?

OTTO: That you would soon see what Germany can do? What do you say now?

CORRIE: I say your manners are no better than they ever were.

THE BEAST: Bite your tongue!

BETSIE: Don't be unkind, Corrie. He doesn't know. We have to show him.

OTTO: What do I not know?

BETSIE: That there is light in the world, and darkness cannot overcome it.

OTTO: You're preaching to me. Do you think that could actually work?

CORRIE: Leave her alone.

BETSIE: Look what they have made of you.

CORRIE: Be quiet, Betsie. Don't.

BETSIE: The light can pierce all darkness, Otto. Even one so deep as yours.

OTTO: And what do you know of a darkness like mine?

BETSIE: I know what lies beyond it.

Beat.

OTTO: Send them to hard labor.

CORRIE: No, please. She's sick. Otto, you can't.

OTTO: CAPTAIN Schwarzhuber!

Take them!

OTTO exits.

THE BEAST: Get them to work!

The Guards herd the Prisoners into the work yard where they clear rocks, breaking them up with pickaxes and loading them into wheelbarrows.

CORRIE: Here. Stay with me, Betsie.

CORRIE and BETSIE work together to break up a rock. BETSIE can barely lift the shovel. BETSIE begins to cry.

BETSIE: I'm so sad for Otto, Corrie.

CORRIE: He's a monster.

BETSIE: And that's why we have to love him. We have to forgive him.

CORRIE: Forgive him? Look around, Betsie. I cannot muster forgiveness here. Not for this. Not for them.

THE BEAST sees BETSIE talking.

THE BEAST: Pick up that shovel! Work!

THE BEAST pushes BETSIE and she falls.

THE BEAST: Get up. Get up, you swine!

CORRIE: Let her be!

THE BEAST strikes BETSIE with her crop and BETSIE falls to the ground.

THE BEAST: Look at her! All of you! This is what happens if you can't work!

CORRIE (unseen by The Beast) picks up the shovel and raises it over her head like a weapon.

BETSIE: *(To CORRIE)*

No! No. Stop!

Other prisoners run to CORRIE and take the shovel from her. BETSIE struggles to her feet.

THE BEAST: Don't let me catch you lazing around again. Arbeit macht frei.

THE BEAST exits. BETSIE's face is covered in blood.

CORRIE: Are you all right? Your face, Betsie.

BETSIE covers the bloody wounds on her head and cries.

BETSIE: She didn't mean it. She doesn't know. I mustn't hate her. I mustn't.

BETSIE is torn between tears and anger.

CORRIE: Get up. I won't let them hurt you.

BETSIE: I have to love my enemy.

CORRIE: I can't. I won't.

BETSIE: Neither can I. Oh but I try, Corrie. I try, and I try and I try--and I can't do it.

But Christ can. Can't he? And he lives in us. Doesn't he?

CORRIE: Doesn't he what? Live inside me? What does that even mean--

BETSIE: Corrie!

CORRIE: The only thing inside me is anger, Betsie. I hate them.

GUARD 2: Work!

BETSIE tries to lift a rock into the cart. She fumbles and falls.

CORRIE: *(to the Guard)*

Please. She's hurt. It's too much.

BETSIE: It's all right, Corrie. I'm fine. I can manage.

CORRIE: Please.

GUARD 2: Get her out of here.

CORRIE helps BETSIE hobble to the barracks. THE BEAST sees them.

THE BEAST: What are you doing? Why aren't you at work?

CORRIE: She's not well. The Guard told me to--

THE BEAST: Maybe she needs a night on the pole.

CORRIE: No. No, please.

CORRIE backs away with BETSIE and enters the barracks. THE BEAST stops at the door and looks around in disgust.

THE BEAST: Back on the line tomorrow. Both of you.

THE BEAST exits and CORRIE lays BETSIE in the bed.

BETSIE: They won't come in here, you know.

CORRIE: Be quiet.

BETSIE: Do you know why they won't come in?

CORRIE: Why?

BETSIE: It's the fleas, Corrie.

CORRIE: What?

BETSIE: They can't stand the fleas. Isn't that funny. They are our little Guards. They stand athwart the door, and the wolves do not come in.

CORRIE: Hush. You need to rest.

Other PRISONERS enter after the day's labor.

GITA: Are you all right, Tante Betsie?

BETSIE: I'm lovely.

JESKE: They didn't hurt you very much did they?

AVIEN runs to hug BETSIE.

BETSIE: Not at all.

CORRIE: Let her be. She needs to sleep.

A NURSE comes to the door.

NURSE: Prisoner 54234?

JESKE: Here I am.

NURSE: Mail.

The NURSE hands JESKE a package.

NURSE: Delivery from the Red Cross. They opened it of course, but I told them it was only crackers. Don't let them find you with it.

The NURSE exits.

TRUDKA: What is it?

JESKE takes it to BETSIE.

JESKE: It's from Pastor Andrei, back home.

JESKE tears open the package and removes a small jar and a bundle of communion wafers.

JESKE: Marmalade!

TRUDKA: Marmalade?

AVIEN: And crackers?

JESKE:	Wait. No. Not crackers. It's . . .
GITA:	Let me see.
JESKE:	Would you do it, Tante Betsie?
BETSIE:	Do it? Do what, dear?
CORRIE:	Leave her alone!
JESKE:	It's the Host. For Communion. Sent with marmalade so they'd think it was only crackers from home.
BETSIE:	Now there's a miracle come among us.

BETSIE takes the small tin, and the PRISONERS gather around and sit at her feet. TRUDKA stands back and looks on from afar.

JESKE:	We have no one else. Will you say the words?
BETSIE:	Me? I'm no priest or pastor. I don't know if it's proper, dear.

JESKE, undeterred, holds out the host for BETSIE and waits. BETSIE looks to CORRIE uncomfortably.

CORRIE:	Lie down, Betsie. You need your rest.
BETSIE:	*(To Jeske)*
	I know not the way, but come. I will try.

As she speaks, MOORMAN is taken to the pole and hung there in agony while OTTO oversees.

BETSIE:	*(reaching to touch Jeske's face)*
	This is his body, broken for us. Even now he is here. He suffers in each of us. He bleeds as we

bleed. He dies as we die--and yet he is neither spent nor consumed.

Do not be afraid, sisters. There is no inch in the whole of Creation over which he does not cry, "Mine!" And that which he claims, he will not fail to make new.

A great good is coming, and we shall all be witness to the thunder of its arrival.

Christ has died. Christ is risen. Christ will come again.

Amen.

The PRISONERS take the bread and eat it as Betsie talks. Finally, TRUDKA joins them.

JESKE: Will you read to us, Betsie?

BETSIE: Of course I will.

BETSIE extends her hand to CORRIE, who hesitantly takes the Bible from around her neck and hands it to Betsie.

BETSIE: Now. Come. Come close. Where were we?

Lights fade. The great clock ticks in the darkness.

YOUNG CORRIE enters, joined by CASPER. CASPER seems to confer with someone offstage, indicating he'll rejoin them shortly.

YOUNG CORRIE: Papa? What's wrong.

CASPER: Come here, Corrie. And listen to me.

YOUNG CORRIE: Is mama, all right?

CASPER: Yes. Yes, I believe that she is.

YOUNG CORRIE: Can I see her?

CASPER: I'm afraid not, my dear Corrie. Look at me now. Your mother has gone away. God has taken her.

YOUNG CORRIE cries as CASPER embraces her.

CORRIE: I don't want her to go away, Papa. I don't want God to take her.

CASPER: I know, my dear. I know. We shall all have to be stronger now. Can you do that?

CORRIE wipes her face and nods.

CASPER: Then be a strong girl for us and go and find your sister. Care for her until I return. We'll talk again later after I've tended to things. I must go.

CASPER exits.

YOUNG CORRIE: Papa wait. If God comes to take you, you have to hide, Papa. I don't want you to go away. Or Betsy, or Willem. If he comes, can we hide, Papa? Papa!

YOUNG CORRIE exits.

CORRIE: Work, sleep, line up, work, sleep . . .

SCENE 5

Guards bang on the door and ring a bell.

GUARD 1: Roll call!

PRISONERS rush out of bed and get into formation. BETSIE can't get out of bed. CORRIE stays with her.

CORRIE: Betsie, what's wrong? Get up.

BETSIE: My legs won't seem to cooperate.

CORRIE: Come on. We have to go.

GITA helps CORRIE get BETSIE out of bed. They drag her outside between them.

THE BEAST: Get in line.

CORRIE: Please. She's sick.

GUARD 1: What's wrong with her?

BETSIE: I'm all right. I'll be fine.

CORRIE: Her legs aren't working right. I don't know

	what's . . .
GUARD 1:	Take her to the infirmary. The rest of you, move!
CORRIE:	Thank you. Thank you.
	Do you hear that, Betsie? No work today. No socks to knit. And no shovels. No Guards. Only a warm bed. Isn't that nice?
BETSIE:	Do you think they have flowers in the infirmary?
CORRIE:	No. I do not.
BETSIE:	I long to see flowers again, Corrie. Wouldn't that be something?

CORRIE and BETSIE hobble to the infirmary and CORRIE puts her into a bed. A NURSE enters.

NURSE:	What's the trouble?
BETSIE:	I just feel a bit weak.
CORRIE:	It's her legs. Circulation problems I think.
NURSE:	Hmmm.
CORRIE:	She'll be okay, won't she?
BETSIE:	Of course I will.
NURSE:	We'll see what can be done.
CORRIE:	She'll take care of you, Betsie. I'll be right here.
NURSE:	Report back to your formation.
CORRIE:	But I have to stay with her. We're sisters.
Nurse:	You may see her again before dinner. Go.

BETSIE:	It's okay, Corrie. Go on.
CORRIE:	I can't. I'm afraid. I don't want to go out there without you, Betsie.
BETSIE:	Go on. I'll be right here. You don't need me.
NURSE:	Out. Don't make them come looking for you.

The ticking of the great clock begins and gradually swells to a manic pace as the scene continues.

CORRIE enters the reality of the camp. Brutality is everywhere. Weeping and wailing fills the air. The smokestack belches smoke. CORRIE watches, walking amid the hellish landscape with growing horror. She runs to a doorway and tries to enter.

CORRIE:	Hide me!
PRISONER 1:	Get away!

She rushes to another nook, but a GUARD sees her and she flees. CORRIE bangs on the closed door of a barracks.

CORRIE: Help!

A crowd of women sweeps her away. CORRIE struggles with them, falls, is trampled. A GUARD threatens her. She flees downstage.

CORRIE:	Hide me! Hide me!
GUARD 2:	Silence! Prisoners do not speak!
CORRIE:	No, no. Leave me alone!
GUARD 1:	Work will set you free! Work!

She hides behind the base of the pole where MOORMAN is hung, near death. She cowers. The GUARDS exit. The PRISONERS exit. The ticking of the great clock ceases.

MOORMAN: *(weakly)*

Watch-woman. Is that you? Come out so I can see you.

CORRIE: Here I am.

MOORMAN: It is you. We did good work, didn't we, watch-woman? Those radios will never speak. Hundreds of them. Thousands. All silent.

And now I have my reward.

CORRIE retreats in horror and exits.

MOORMAN: Where are you going, watch-woman? Don't leave me. Don't leave me.

CORRIE stumbles to the infirmary.

CORRIE: Betsie?

BETSIE: Corrie, I'm so glad you're here.

CORRIE: You're hot. Burning up. Did she give you any medicine.

BETSIE: A bit of vitamin, I think.

CORRIE: Vitamin? You've got to get better. I need you. You've got to get better and we've got to get out of here.

BETSIE: There are so many sick girls here, Corrie, so many on the threshold of heaven. I mustn't leave them.

CORRIE: What are you talking about? What about me, Betsie. I can't do this without you.

BETSIE: Yes, you can. He will help you.

CORRIE: Who? Who, Betsie?

BETSIE: You know who.

CORRIE: Where is he, Betsie. I can't see him. There is no god here.

BETSIE: But he is, Corrie. He is. Can I tell you something?

CORRIE: Of course. You can tell me anything.

BETSIE: We will be released soon. It's nearly Christmas, and we'll be released before the year is up. I've seen it.

CORRIE: Released? What are you saying?

BETSIE: We will leave on a great journey, across many miles. And your bed will not be your own. It will be years before you can rest.

CORRIE: Nurse? Nurse, Betsie's not well. There's something wrong.

BETSIE: I see a fair place. A camp like this one but . . . transfigured. Flowers everywhere. A dark place made bright. A winter place grown spring. A place where all these girls can learn how to love again. You will teach them, Corrie. You must.

CORRIE: I don't understand. You're scaring me. I'm afraid, Betsie. I'm so afraid.

BETSIE: You said that to Papa once. And do you remember what Papa told us?

CORRIE:	Papa's dead.
BETSIE:	He told us about the train station. Remember? We'll have what we need just at the moment we need it. We'll wait for our ticket.
CORRIE:	Look around you, Betsie. Papa's not here. This isn't a train station. They're pushing girls into a gas chamber over there! They're shoving bodies into an oven. They aren't even trying to hide it! And the children, Betsie. They murder children! How long until they come for little Avien? I can't bear it. I haven't the right to bear it. Or to love them. Or to forgive them. I can't do it! I won't do it! I won't.
BETSIE:	He can. He does. He will help you.
CORRIE:	I don't care! I don't care! Maybe HE can bear it, but I can't, Betsie! Don't you see? I don't want his ticket. I won't take it from him. I won't get onto his train. I won't do it! I won't go.

The NURSE enters.

NURSE:	That's long enough. If they see you in here, you'll be in the bunker. You can come again before work in the morning.
Corrie:	I have to go.
BETSIE:	On your journey?
CORRIE:	There is no journey, Betsie. We have come to the place where all roads end.
BETSIE:	Then it's a fit place for a beginning.

CORRIE: I'll come again in the morning. Get your sleep.

CORRIE exits. In the courtyard, she walks past MOORMAN hung on the pole. The throat of the crematorium vomits smoke above them.

MOORMAN: Please. Help me, watch-woman. Some water. Don't leave me.

CORRIE runs to the barracks. The other prisoners part and she throws herself onto the bed. The prisoners gather around her.

GITA: Is Tante Betsie all right?

JESKE: Where is she? She hasn't died has she?

CORRIE: She's sick. She's very sick. Leave me alone.

AVIEN: Can we go and see Tante Betsie?

Several of the PRISONERS begin to cry.

JESKE: Will you read to us, Corrie?

GITA: Would you, please?

CORRIE: Read to you?

JESKE: If Tante Betsie's not here, why not?

CORRIE: I can't.

TRUDKA: Have you lost it?

CORRIE draws the Bible from around her neck. The PRISONERS gather around her and sit at her feet.

JESKE: Read to us, Tante Corrie. To Avien.

AVIEN: Read like Tante Betsie.

Reluctantly, CORRIE opens the Bible and begins to read in a flat, emotionless voice.

CORRIE: "Blessed be God, the Father of all mercies and comfort, who comforts us in our trouble, that we may comfort others.

For as the sufferings of Christ abound in us, so our consolation abounds through Him.

As CORRIE reads, BETSIE crawls out of bed and goes to the other women in the infirmary, tending them gently.

GITA: Go on, Tante Corrie. Read.

CORRIE & BETSIE: If I am afflicted, it is for your consolation and salvation. And if I am comforted, it is for your consolation and salvation.

And my hope for you is steadfast, because I know that as you partake of great suffering, so also you will partake of great consolation.

MOORMAN is lowered from the pole and dragged away, dead. CORRIE speaks as to the audience.

CORRIE: For we want you to know of the trouble that befell us.

BETSIE: That we were burdened beyond measure, beyond our strength.

CORRIE: We despaired of all things.

In the infirmary, BETSIE helps another woman out of a wheelchair and into her own bed, then she slumps into the chair and becomes motionless. CORRIE drops the Bible. AVIEN picks it up and hands it to her, then hugs her.

CORRIE: We carried the sentence of death, so that we should not trust in ourselves, but in God who raises the dead. And in him we have hidden our hope of deliverance.

AVIEN: What does it mean, Tante Corrie? I don't understand.

CORRIE: Neither do I. Neither do I.

CORRIE rolls into her bed and cries. The others follow, comforting CORRIE. Lights down.

The ticking of the great clock. YOUNG BETSIE enters.

CASPER: *(unseen)*

Betsie? Come here, child. Come to your papa.

A brilliant beam of light shoots across the stage. YOUNG BETSIE slowly crosses the stage into the light and exits.

SCENE 6

The bells ring for roll call. PRISONERS *get up and rush outside and into formation.* CORRIE *rushes to the infirmary instead.*

GUARD: *(offstage)*

Get in line! Ranks of five!

CORRIE: Betsie? Betsie?

CORRIE *finds the bed empty. She rushes around the room checking the other beds.*

NURSE: What are you doing? Get out of here.

CORRIE: Please. Where's my sister? Where's Betsie? Where have they taken her?

NURSE: She's not here. I'm sorry.

CORRIE: What? No! Where is she?

NURSE: You'd best get out of here. I'll call the Guards.

CORRIE *runs to the crematorium. A stack of bodies are piled against the wall. She overturns the top one revealing green colors. It's* BETSIE.

CORRIE: No. No. No. Don't leave me. We've got to get out. I'm getting you out of here. Do you hear? Come on!

CORRIE pulls the body away, drags it center stage and tries to lift and carry it. She cannot. She kneels and gathers BETSIE into her arms.

At the periphery of the stage, like shadows, the other prisoners look on and hum a mournful hymn: "O Come, O Come, Emmanuel." No words.

CORRIE: Why would you take her. Why?

Come on, Betsie. We're going home, remember? You said we'd be released.

They can't have you. No. They can't, they can't.

GITA extends her hand to CORRIE to pull her away.

GITA: It's time.

The prisoners take BETSIE's body. CORRIE tries to follow, but falls to her knees as she watches BETSIE carried away. The walls of the crematorium roll away revealing a monstrous iron oven. The oven door is opened and radiant light streams from its mouth, piercing all darkness. The light is not fire like, or filled with terror, but is instead of a great beauty.

BETSIE is fed into the light. CORRIE stares into the heart of the oven, transfixed by the mysterious beauty of the light until the oven door closes and the entire set is enveloped in smoke and darkness. The great clock chimes ominously and then ceases.

Silence is kept.

When the smoke clears, THE BEAST enters.

THE BEAST: Prisoner Ten Boom?

CORRIE: What? Did you say my name?

THE BEAST: Are you Cornelia Ten Boom?

CORRIE: I am.

THE BEAST: Get up. Come with me.

CORRIE follows the GUARD into an office. Another GUARD sits behind a desk.

GUARD 2: Prisoner 66730, Ten Boom?

CORRIE: Yes? What's going on?

CORRIE is handed a bundle of clothes. The GUARD stamps a piece of paper.

GUARD 2: Have you been mistreated during your sentence here?

CORRIE: What?

THE BEAST: Answer the question!

CORRIE: No.

GUARD 2: Have you witnessed any mistreatment of prisoners here?

CORRIE: N . . . no.

GUARD 2: Good. Sign here.

CORRIE signs the paper.

THE BEAST: Your sentence is complete. You are free to go, fraulein.

CORRIE: Go? Go where?

THE BEAST: That is for you to decide.

CORRIE walks outside. The gates open. She steps through and the gates shut behind her. She looks around helplessly. The other PRISONERS press themselves against the fence and reach out to her.

GITA: Goodbye, Tante Corrie.

JESKE: Remember us.

CORRIE: Gita, I don't know where to go. I don't know what to do.

GITA: You have to go. God bless you.

JESKE: Go, Tante Corrie.

AVIEN: Goodbye, Tante Corrie.

CORRIE removes the Bible from her neck and gives it to AVIEN.

TRUDKA: Go on.

GITA: I release you.

JESKE: I release you.

TRUDKA: I release you.

Any other prisoners on stage say "I release you."

The sounds of planes and war sweep across the stage. Two RED CROSS WORKERS enter and wrap CORRIE in a coat, helping her offstage. As the lights dim, the prisoners fall to the ground one by one. The RED CROSS WORKERS return and the lights come up on the camp. Motionless bodies are everywhere. The workers walk among the dead. One stirs. A worker picks up AVIEN.

RED CROSS WORKER 1: She lives!

The worker rushes her offstage as the sound of a radio crackles to life and the stage goes dark. As the radio voice speaks, the lights reveal YOUNG CORRIE, *swallowed by the Red Cross Coat. She stands centerstage, lonely, and looks around her, as if appraising the ruin of a great city. As the radio address ends, she sheds the coat and takes a tentative step forward as the lights fade to darkness.*

RADIO: *(Truman's voice in the darkness)*

They have violated our churches, destroyed our homes, corrupted our children, and murdered our loved ones. Yet through God's help we have been freed of the evil forces which have imprisoned the bodies and broken the lives of millions upon millions of free-born people. Now we must seek to bind up the wounds of a suffering world.

SCENE 7

Silence broods over the darkness of the stage until CORRIE *enters. She considers the set as the lights reveal the Beje briefly, a tattered Reich Flag briefly, a barracks, the great clock.*

She walks through the empty Beje, touching precious objects. She picks up a picture from the mantle and embraces it.

CORRIE: I miss you, Papa.

PICKWICK **enters.**

PICKWICK: As I live and breath. Corrie ten Boom.

CORRIE: Pickwick!

CORRIE *and* PICKWICK *embrace.*

CORRIE: What a joy to see you. How are you?

PICKWICK: I am . . . here. Since the war ended I'm putting things back together.

CORRIE: Aren't we all.

PICKWICK: What of old Casper?

CORRIE:	Papa didn't last more than a few days. It was a blessing, I think.
PICKWICK:	And your sister? What about Betsie?
CORRIE:	*(shaking her head)*
	With Papa. Willem too.
PICKWICK:	*(sits down)*
	Oh, Corrie. What will become of us?
CORRIE:	I don't know, Pickwick. But what about them. What about those poor people we left in the hiding place?
PICKWICK:	They climbed out through a window in the night. Can you believe it?
CORRIE:	Then it wasn't for nothing, was it?
PICKWICK:	In the two years you hid people here, how many did you save? Four hundred? Six hundred? More? That's far from nothing, Corrie.
	And anyway, kindness is never for nothing, even if nothing is all that ever comes of it.
CORRIE:	You sound like Betsie.
PICKWICK:	Why thank you.
CORRIE:	Do you know they tell me it was all a clerical error.
PICKWICK:	What's that?
CORRIE:	At Ravensbruck. It was a simple clerical error.

> They never meant me to leave at all. I was to go into the ovens with the rest of them.

PICKWICK: But here we are.

CORRIE: Yes, here we are.

PICKWICK: And now what?

The clock begins to tick. CORRIE *is isolated in light.*

YOUNG CORRIE: *(offstage)*

> Listen.

BETSIE: *(offstage)*

> Listen.

CASPER: *(offstage)*

> Watch.

CORRIE: I hear you. All of you. All times. All places. Here. There. Then. And now.

The silence is filled, and it can remain silent no longer.

The clock stops and the light dissipates.

PICKWICK: Corrie?

CORRIE: I've seen such hatred. And not only in the Nazis, Pickwick. I found it in myself too. Like a coal in my chest, desperate to get out and burn someone. It's still there, hot and smoldering.

> How can it ever be quenched?

> By love maybe? By forgiveness? If I can muster it.

PICKWICK: Forgiveness? That is a hard pill to swallow.

CORRIE: But that's the thing isn't it? That's what Papa and Betsie were always trying to make us understand. Forgiveness is never efficient. It mustn't make any sense in the economy of human understanding.

Forgiveness must be a scandal if it's to have any power at all.

You see, I've stared into the great darkness, Pickwick. I'm a witness. And if I'm to be a good one, I must testify.

PICKWICK: And what will you say?

CORRIE: That I've seen what lies beyond it. Just like Betsie did. Just like Papa.

Pickwick: And what is that?

CORRIE: It's him.

The Prince of Clerical Errors, the Master of Marmalade, the Father of Fleas, the Man of All Sorrows, who sets watches and galaxies spinning--he was there too, in every one of us: Christus Victor.

And he is here still. I cannot stand and watch any longer.

CORRIE picks up BETSIE's teapot and considers it.

CORRIE: I must go back. To Germany.

PICKWICK: What in the world for?

CORRIE: It's what Betsie wanted, and she was right.

PICKWICK: My dear Corrie, your father and grandfather, shone a light in our city for a hundred years.

And now, here it is again. What shall we do first?

CORRIE walks around the room in thought.

CORRIE: We'll start with windowboxes.

PICKWICK: What?

CORRIE: Like Betsie used to do. We must turn the camp into something beautiful.

There will be flowers. Flowers everywhere.

CORRIE goes to a chest in the corner and pulls out a swath of bright green cloth.

CORRIE: Ah, there she is . . . what was it she said? A dark place made bright. A winter place grown spring.

A place transfigured.

PICKWICK: So be it. I know just the people to talk to.

PICKWICK exits.

CORRIE: Oh how I miss you.

CORRIE lays the scarf on the table and exits. OTTO enters the Beje in shadow, his face hidden from the audience. He examines the room, picks up BETSIE's scarf and considers it, then exits as . . .

SCENE 8

Corrie and Pickwick enter the train station.

PICKWICK: I've spoken with my friends in the reconstruction department and they are waiting for us there. The train for Berlin leaves in just a few minutes. Wait here a moment, dear. I'll fetch our tickets.

CORRIE: Thank you, Pickwick.

Pickwick places Corrie's heavy leather suitcase on the stage exactly where it was in the beginning of Act I and exits. Corrie sees it and stares, as if it's unlocked a memory.

Otto enters.

OTTO: Corrie? Corrie ten Boom?

CORRIE: Yes. May I help you?

OTTO: It's me. Do you remember?

Corrie is silent and cold.

Otto: *(nervously)*

It's Otto.

Corrie: I have not forgotten.

Otto: Things have been so confusing lately, with the end of the war.

Corrie looks on coldly.

Otto: Is your sister with you?

Corrie: No. She is not.

Otto: For some reason, I've never been able to forget what Betsie said to me. That a light had come into the world, a light that could pierce any darkness. Something like that. It sticks with me, isn't that odd?

May I tell you something?

Now that the war is over, I believe forgiveness is the only way forward. Don't you think so?

Corrie is silent.

Otto: Isn't that right?

Otto extends his hand. Corrie backs away from it.

The ticking of the great clock. Casper, Young Betsie, and Young Corrie enter.

Young Corrie: Papa, Papa, where are we going!

Young Betsie: A train! Are we going on the train?

Young Corrie: Is Mama coming with us?

CASPER: Enough questions. Come with me.

CASPER gives a ticket to YOUNG BETSIE. She runs to the attendant laughing. He takes the ticket and she boards with a last look back.

YOUNG BETSIE: Come on, Corrie!

CASPER and YOUNG CORRIE approach the attendant.

TRAIN ATTENDANT: Tickets?

CASPER: Here you are, Corrie.

YOUNG CORRIE takes the ticket and hands it to the TRAIN ATTENDANT.

CASPER: Good girl. It's a long way to go, now. Catch up with your sister. No time to waste.

YOUNG CORRIE boards the train. CORRIE stares after them in amazement. The clock ceases. CASPER pauses and turns toward CORRIE expectantly.

PICKWICK enters and holds a ticket out for CORRIE.

CORRIE: What's this?

PICKWICK: This one's yours. No time to waste.

CORRIE: What did you say?

PICKWICK: For the train.

CORRIE stares at the ticket. And then at OTTO. Finally she takes the ticket and places it in her coat. Then, slowly, stiffly, extends her hand to OTTO who shakes it.

OTTO: Thank you, Fraulein Ten Boom. I've seen such darkness, you know?

CORRIE: Yes. I know.

OTTO: But there is no darkness so deep . . .

CORRIE: . . . that he is not deeper still.

OTTO: Goodbye then. Auf weidersehen.

OTTO exits.

PICKWICK: Who was that? He looked familiar.

CORRIE stares after OTTO.

PICKWICK: Are you all right, Corrie? What's wrong? What did he say?

CORRIE regains control of herself.

CORRIE: Come. Our train is boarding.

PICKWICK boards the train. CORRIE hesitates. She looks down and considers the suitcase, approaching it thoughtfully, then plucks it up and hefts its weight in her hand, lifting it easily. She extends the ticket toward the train-attendant. He takes it. Tears it. Hands it back.

CORRIE turns and looks after OTTO, then looks at CASPER who smiles at her before boarding the train.

CORRIE: All aboard, then.

CORRIE draws in a deep breath.

CORRIE: And off we go.

CORRIE steps onto the train and it rumbles offstage. The great clock ticks along in perfect synchronicity.

THE END

Also from
Rabbit Room Press

The Battle of Franklin
by A. S. Peterson

The Last Sweet Mile
by Allen Levi

Everlasting Is the Past
by Walter Wangerin, Jr.

The World According to Narnia
by Jonathan Rogers

www.RabbitRoom.com

www.ingramcontent.com/pod-product-compliance
Lightning Source LLC
Chambersburg PA
CBHW020935090426
42736CB00010B/1147